Swiridoff

Portraits from Ge Intellect

rman

ual Life

Neske

The Story of this Book

The undertaking of which these pages are the record was an adventurous one, both on a physical and on a mental level, growing more so, in a number of ways, as it neared completion.

The first problem to be overcome was that of selection, of limiting the material to proportions suitable for one volume; this was no easy task, for any choice of less than a hundred names as representative of intellectual life in Germany must necessarily be subjective, and hence arguable.

I therefore consider it idle to attempt to refute any criticism of my selection; in fact, I freely concede in advance that such criticism is justified—though with the reservation that my choice be taken for what it is; one of many possible ones. If, however, I am accused of conjuring up in these pictures a number of incompatible worlds, my answer is that this is exactly what I meant to do. For if I must abandon any claim to having made a complete and definitive selection, I have nevertheless attempted to mirror the German intellectual scene in all its breadth and variety.

In making this attempt I found myself a traveller in a realm of contrasts, moments of discouragement alternating with moments of exhilaration. After being accustomed to having one's favourite and familiar works of literature arranged in neat rows round one, in their leather, cloth or paper bindings, what a difference it is to come face to face with their creators! When one does, the seeming harmony of these volumes, crowded cheek by jowl on their shelves, is soon dispelled and replaced by "the strife of things, harsh in real space", as Schiller has it. On my travels I found, however, that the men of letters whom I visited, despite the differences in their temperaments and the mental climates in which they live, are united in some mysterious way by a common spiritual bond. It has been my aim to make this community of spirit apparent in my pictures; and each portrait embodies its own genesis, which for me is inseparable from it.

Porto Ronco. A house without a nameplate on the steep shores of Lago Maggiore. The door is opened to me, and I am asked to wait in an enormous room flooded with sunlight. On the walls, pictures by Manet, Degas, Monet; and the carpets I am treading are such as normally adorn the walls of art galleries. Books everywhere. A desk covered in papers, magazines and letters. My host comes in, and I seem to imagine his words of greeting to be: "All Quiet On The Western Front"! This, then, is Remarque, by whom Germany, and indeed the whole world, was split into two camps with his anti-war novel in the late twenties.

A gentleman of the old stamp of whom, with his little more than sixty years, it is hard to believe that he is really *the* Remarque! Indeed, many years have passed since his book was devoured by an eager public, being translated into more than a hundred languages within a few years. He recalls the time when, as a sport columnist, he wrote the novel in less than a month, mostly at night, but did not find a publisher.

Back again to Wilflingen, to meet Ernst Jünger, the complete antithesis of Remarque, and author of "In the Steel Storm".

The two are worlds apart! Here, too, are books galore, in corridors, in rooms and on the staircase. In among them a quantity of dried sea-creatures, reptiles, baskets full of seashells large and small. In one of the corridors, we stop before a wall of books that reaches to

5

the ceiling. As my eyes rove over the titles, Jünger says: "Here, look; two thousand books just on beetles!" My skin begins to crawl! Never before have I learnt so much about the denizens of the deep in so short a time; I felt almost as if it were Neptune himself I was calling on. My interest was far from being feigned, but at the same time I could not repress a shudder. As I take my leave, some dangerously overhanging branches are being removed from a giant elm across the road outside the residence of the von Stauffenberg family, one member of which had taken upon himself the task of planting the bomb intended to kill Hitler, on 20th July 1944; I hear Jünger tell the workmen to let him know of any little creatures they may find in the wood…

Wood has been a dominant factor in the life of Hap Grieshaber, whom I visited some months later. At his house up on the Achalm I was told that he had gone down to the veneer factory of Messrs. Danzer in Reutlingen, where he was carving the battering-ram intended as a decoration for the new town hall. This is just what I want. It is Saturday; the factory is deserted. The porter takes me to the shop where Hap is at work. He neither hears nor sees me approach; he is lying on the enormous block of wood, which is a good fifty feet long by three feet wide, attacking it with hammer, chisel and knife, like an eagle wrestling with a huge snake. This seeming life-and-death battle continues for a while, until he raises his head and notices my presence. He wipes the perspiration from his brow and greets me with a roar of Homeric laughter, a mixture of pleasure and self-consciousness. "There you are", he says, pointing to the huge tree-trunk, "it's coming on"; then sweeps the shavings away with his hand, and falls upon his victim with renewed vigour. Not all of my sittings went off as smoothly and informally. On another occasion, a visit to Munich was preceded by a number of letters and telephone calls, which finally elicited a date on which I might come, although an interview could not be promised. I arrive at my destination on time; Professor Mössbauer's secretary informs me that he is not there, and that she knows nothing about his whereabouts. I stop a student in the corridor and ask him. The professor? Yes, he is there, all right, in the library, he has just been sitting opposite him. I go back to the secretary; very good, she will send for him. About half an hour after the time of my arrival, he comes, a tall, good-looking man who says: "Please make it quick; I'm busy". I hurriedly make my preparations, put a chair outside on the landing, where the light is stronger, and ask him to be seated. Then the telephone rings; he speaks for a quarter of an hour, apparently in a good humour, then returns, however, in a poor one. I bid him sit down again, and this time have soon done, whereupon he disappears. My assistant looks at me and asks: "Was that what they call the Mössbauer effect?"

Diessen, luckily, is quite near Munich; I go on to visit Carl Orff there. Music played on half a dozen instruments, combined with recitation and singing; a flood of words and music pours over me. He plays on the grand piano at which, as a young man, he composed the Carmina Burana, and recites from Agnes Bernauer. At one point he quotes from Hölderlin's Hyperion: "reconciliation in the midst of strife"; this is not a bad watchword for my rendezvous the following day in Hamburg, with Rudolf Augstein, the editor of 'Der Spiegel'.

"Berlin is worth a journey", they say; it took me six until I had accomplished my mission there. I call on Günter Grass at noon on a rainy day in early December; I wait for a while in his study, where Western furnishings are arranged with Eastern sparseness. The floor of bare boards without a carpet, the bookshelves plain. The books do not include his own—maybe his children are old enough to read... A half-finished drawing stands on an easel; my wife expresses the hope that he will one day devote himself entirely to art. Then he comes in; and it is a pleasure to talk to him. On the window-sill is a monstrous parrot, a contraption of his own making; he presses a button, and a parrot-like voice announces from a hidden tape-recorder the victory of the Social Democrats in the coming elections. Our leave-taking is brief but cordial; he has to get on with the cooking, which he always does on Sundays—this time it is roast goose. In any case, it was high time I left, as I had a call to pay next door, in a neglected old block of flats. On the fifth floor, I find the door I am looking for, with an almost illegible nameplate:

Johnson. I ring. Uwe Johnson opens the door. We go in. Behind the door is a huge poster showing Khrushchev and Ulbricht in a fraternal embrace, on the wall a portrait of Brecht; that is the sum total of the decoration. Apart from that, only a table, a chair, a bookcase, a typewriter and a huge skylight, through which the dull December daylight falls on the writer sitting there in his leather jacket and tie. I try to make conversation, but am at the wrong address; hardly a sentence can I wring from him. So I ask him to go on writing, without taking any notice of me. There is a knock at the door, and an unexpected bonus enters, in the shape of Martin Walser; with him conversation is not exactly easy, but easier. They are both in a hurry to leave; they help us carry the cameras downstairs and, while we wait for a taxi, disappear next door—to dine on Grass's roast goose.

And so it goes on, little episode after little episode, picture after picture. Pictures of the past, too. I was deeply moved when Martin Heidegger at Zähringen showed me a photo of Nietzsche and a daguerrotype of Schelling in old age; they prepared me particularly well for my next encounter, I thought, as I left Freiburg for Basle. To Jaspers, too, I was no stranger; I knew from an earlier meeting of his great love for Heidelberg, for many years the place where he lived and taught, and I was glad to be able to give a sick man pleasure with a shot of his beloved Heidelberg taken from the heights of the so-called Philosophers' Walk.

Shortly afterwards I am in Marbach-on-Neckar, on the top floor of the Schiller Museum, where the walls slope steeply towards the ridge of the roof. There, bent low over his desk, sits Eduard Berend, a man of over eighty; since his return from exile in Geneva some years ago, he has been living here, completing his life's work of research into the writings of Jean Paul. It is good to think that such people still exist, and a sad thought that they may be the last of their kind. They never know the fleeting glory of popular fame, nor do they seek it; their voices would be drowned in the noise of the outside world, and they continue their work in quiet seclusion.

The Max Planck Institute at Göttingen; I am paying a visit to Otto Hahn, one of the founding fathers of the atomic age. He shows me to a chair with a paternal gesture, and makes conversation easy for me. He recalls how he finished his chemistry studies within a few semesters. Nowadays things are different; people study for as much as nine years, at the end of which time they ought really to begin all over again. In his day chemical research had been a comparatively haphazard business; you mixed this and that together, hoping the result would be of some use. He gets up and takes me to see one of the walls of his study, covered with photographs of his friends; the whole scientific revolution that took place between the late nineteenth century and modern times comes alive for me–from Mme. Curie, Einstein, Bohr, Planck, Ilse Meitner to Heisenberg and Weizsäcker. I tell him of the book I am working on. "Excellent idea", he interrupts me, "but you mustn't forget my friend Max Born". I tell him I have just been to Bad Pyrmont, but did not manage to meet Professor Born. "That I can well believe", he says with a knowing smile, picks up the telephone, dials a number, and within a couple of minutes I have an appointment with Max Born for the next morning at the Sonne Hotel in Göttingen.

My saga began with one unique and unforgettable encounter, and ended with another. One of my first commitments was the meeting with Walter Gropius at the Frankfurter Hof Hotel in Frankfurt; one of the last, at the same place, was with Nelly Sachs, on the occasion of her being awarded the German Publishers' Peace Prize. Gropius– his name already a legend, the architect who caught the spirit of his age in shapes of stone, steel and glass; and Nelly Sachs–the poetess who caught and held in words the sufferings her age had traced in sand, smoke and ashes.

Let me conclude this account with my thanks to all those whom I was privileged to meet while engaged on my task. I remember the moment when I left to fly back westwards from Berlin after taking the last portrait in this series; it was that of Dietrich Fischer-Dieskau, the master of the German lied, which still forms a bond between Germany, East and West, and the rest of the world. This was a moment tinged with the sadness of parting, and with sorrow at the separation whose reflection is also to be found in this book.

Paul Swiridoff

Walter Gropius

Walter Gropius was born in Berlin in 1883, studied architecture, and in 1908 became chief assistant to Peter Behrens in the latter's office in Berlin, where Mies van der Rohe and le Corbusier were learning their trade at the same time. At the age of 28 Gropius designed the Fagus works at Alfeld-on-Leine, making architectural history with his use of steel and glass. In 1914 there followed the office block at the Werkbund exhibition in Cologne.

At the end of the First World War, on the suggestion of Henry van de Velde, Gropius was called to Weimar, where he united the local school of arts and crafts with the college of art to form a national institution known as the Bauhaus, the task of which was to be to combine art, craft and technology, and to build in a way which was both functional and appropriate to the materials used. In 1925 Gropius moved to Dessau, together with the Bauhaus, which under his direction since 1919 had become a unique centre of creative activity. Feininger, Marcks, Klee and Kandinsky were among the teachers whom he summoned to work with him.

In 1934 Gropius moved to England, then to the U.S.A. Gropius is Professor Emeritus of Harvard University; he holds a number of honorary degress and other awards. His work in both the Old World and the New has made his name as an architect legendary. "The architectonic quality of a modern building depends on the convincing expressive power of its organic proportions. We must aim at clear, organic structures in harmony with the present-day world of machines and rapid vehicles, free from ephemeral and dishonest effects which obscure the intrinsic shapes of buildings."

Hans Scharoun

Hans Scharoun, born in
Bremen in 1893, studied in
Berlin from 1912 to 1914.
He established himself as an
architect and, in 1925, was
invited to teach at the Breslau
Academy of Art. In the twenties he was one of the architects
of the famous "Weissenhof-
siedlung" in Stuttgart, the
building exhibition "Wohnung
und Werkraum" in Breslau
and of the housing estate
Siemensstadt in Berlin. In 1945
Scharoun became head of
the Department of Public
Works and Housing of the
City of Berlin and with his
team, the "Berlin Kollektiv",
developed a bold plan for the
reconstruction of Berlin.
From 1946 to 1958 he was
professor of town planning
at Berlin Technical University.
He participated successfully
in competitions, built point-
blocks of flats in Stuttgart,
schools at Luenen and
Marl and the new Berlin
Philharmonic Hall.
Scharoun is President of the
Berlin Academy of Fine Arts.

13

Ludwig Mies van der Rohe

Together with Wright, le Corbusier and Gropius, Mies van der Rohe is ranked among the most influential architects of the first half of this century. Born at Aachen in 1886, he was encouraged in his first steps towards his future profession by his father, a master bricklayer who owned a small stonemason's business. He learned to draw by designing stucco ornaments. After a spell with an architect in Berlin, he was apprenticed to the designer Bruno Paul. In 1907 he broke out for a while on his own, and then joined Peter Behrens, at that time Germany's most creative architect; the years he spent with Behrens were crucial ones in Mies's development. From now on he strove to perfect a modern type of architecture combining neo-classical severity, purity of outline, perfect proportions, elegance of detail and dignity of expression. After the First World War he more and more developed his own unmistakable style. The buildings which he designed during this period reflect the forward-looking spirit of post-war Berlin; among them is the memorial to Karl Lieb-knecht and Rosa Luxemburg, which was later destroyed by the Nazis. In 1927, he directed the building of the Weissenhof development in Stuttgart, commissioned by the Werkbund and planned by a team of Europe's leading architects; in 1929 he designed the German pavilion at the International Exhibition in Barcelona. In 1930, at the request of Walter Gropius, Mies took over the post of director of the Bauhaus, which he later moved to Berlin. When Hitler came to power in 1933, Mies decided to close the "Bauhaus", and in 1937 emigrated to the U.S.A., where his influence grew so rapidly that the following year he was offered a chair at the Illinois Institute of Technology in Chicago. Passionately concerned as he is with purity of form, Mies van der Rohe's architecture exemplifies the principle that the creative imagination is best employed in seeking the simplest solution. Mies van der Rohe is a member of the Order Pour le Mérite for Arts and Science.

Wassili Luckhardt

Wassili Luckhardt, the son of a manufacturer, was born in 1889 in Berlin, despite his Slavonic first name, which he owes to a godfather. After studying architecture in Berlin, Munich and Dresden, and five years as a soldier during the war, he began his career as a free-lance architect, together with his brother Hans. He introduced into Germany the principle of steel and reinforced concrete framing, in a series of detached and terraced houses built in the Schorlemer Allee in Dahlem, a suburb of Berlin, between 1924 and 1928. In a model built for the Reichsforschungsgesellschaft (National Research Association) in 1929, he demonstrated for the first time the construction technique known today as box frame construction. His "Telschow Building" in the Potsdamer Platz, of the same date, attracted considerable attention with the complete innovation of a façade entirely of glass. In 1923 Hans and Wassili Luckhardt, together with other architects, formed the group known as "The Ring", which had a great influence on the development of modern architectural design. Because of their views on modern architecture, the two brothers were unable to pursue their profession during the years 1933–1945, but they remained in Berlin, supporting themselves by means of various activities, including a number of inventions.

Their first success after the Second World War was the "Hall of the City of Berlin" at the "Constructa" exhibition in Hanover in 1951, which brought them widespread recognition.

Since the death of his brother in 1954, Wassili Luckhardt has worked alone. He participated in the demonstration of modern architecture in the Hansa Quarter of Berlin, being responsible, together with Hubert Hoffmann, for a four-storey block of flats.

With the new parliament building in Bremen, Luckhardt sought a new solution to the difficult problem of harmonising contemporary architecture with venerable buildings of the past.

Egon Eiermann

Egon Eiermann, the architect, was born in September 1904 at Neuendorf, near Berlin. He studied under Hans Poelzig at the Berlin Institute of Technology from 1923 to 1927, during which time he designed film and theatre sets, and furniture. After taking his finals, he became a free-lance architect, and built his first dwelling-houses. In 1938 came his first important commission for an industrial building. In the summer of 1947 he was appointed to a chair of architecture unico loco at the Institute of Technology in Karlsruhe, and pupils of his include a great number of successful architects of today. Since 1947 Eiermann has been responsible for the design of all kinds of architectural work. Particularly well-known examples of buildings completed to his plans are the German pavilion at the World Exhibition in Brussels in 1958 (for which Sep Ruf was also partly responsible), the Kaiser Wilhelm Memorial Church in Berlin (1957 – 1963), and the German Embassy in Washington (1958–1964). Besides his large buildings, he has also produced numerous chair designs, showing the universality of his work and his liking for, and attention to, detail. Eiermann has received an honorary doctorate of Berlin Technical University, and has won a number of awards for design at home and abroad.

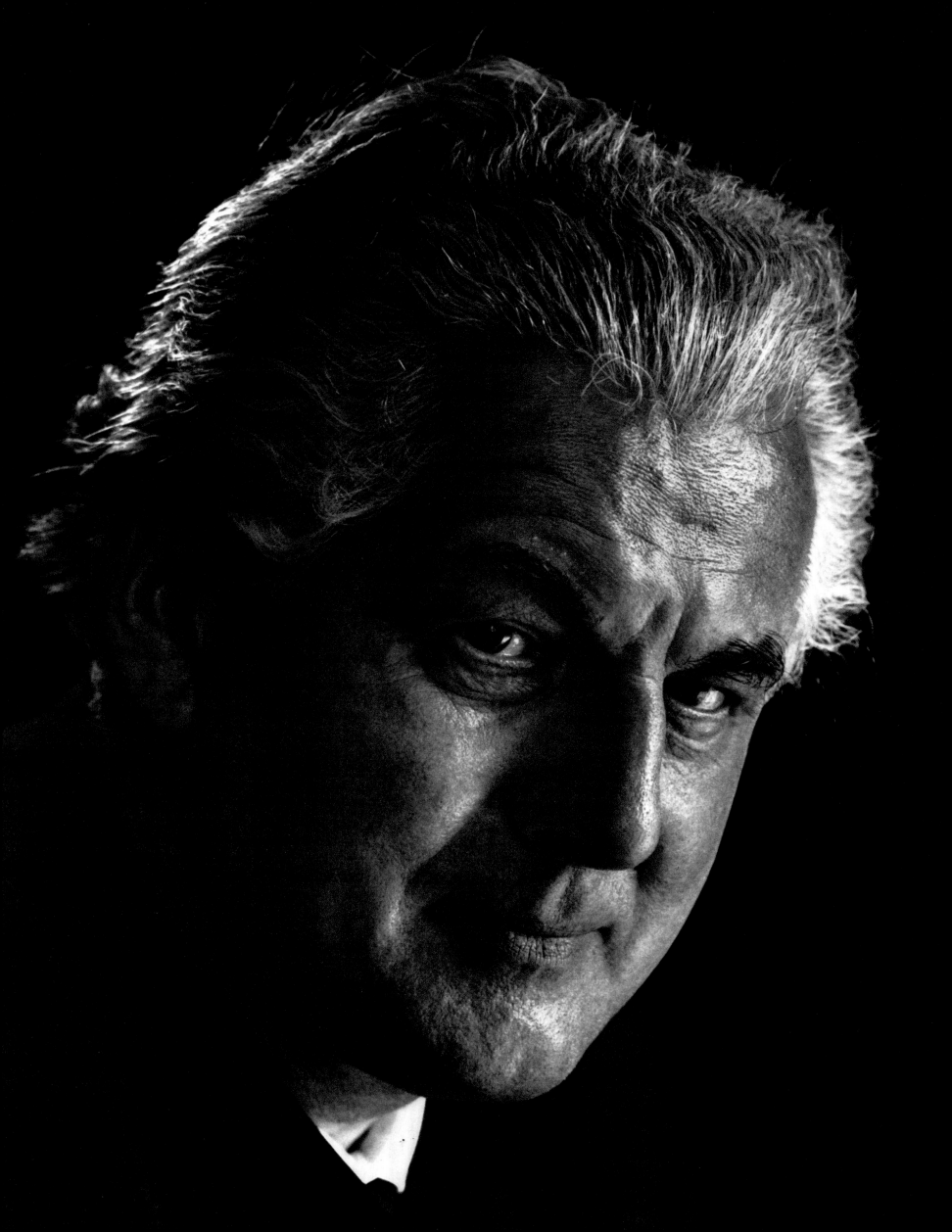

67-2857

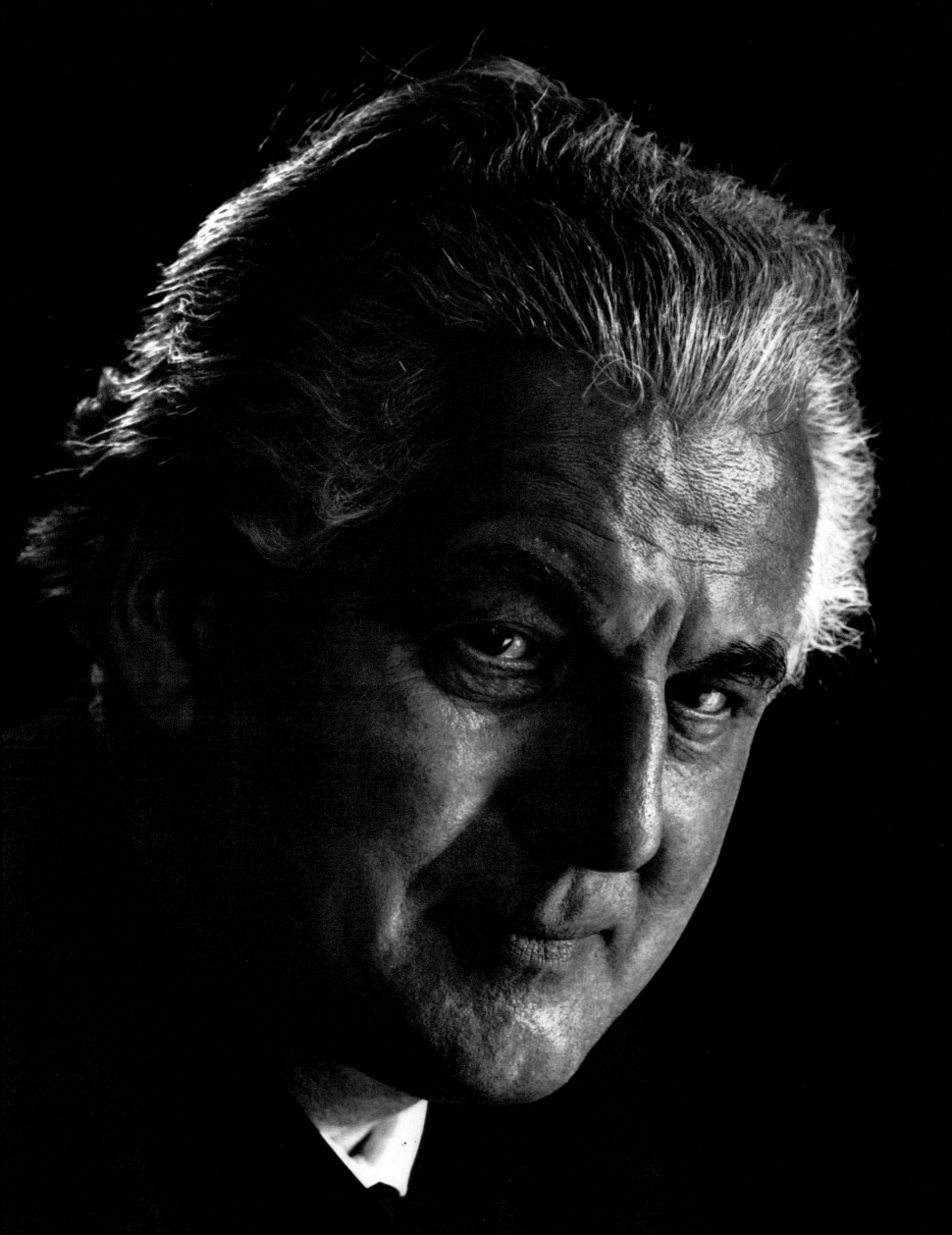

Sep Ruf

Sep Ruf, who was born in Munich in 1908, is one of the most important architects Germany has produced since the Second World War. The first of Ruf's main works, which include the State Bank of Bavaria and the Art Academy at Nuremberg, were produced subsequent to his appointment to the latter institution in 1947. In 1953 he obtained an appointment to the Munich Art Academy, of which he was president from 1958 to 1961. Here he designed the new American Consulate-General, the Max Planck Institute for Physics and Astrophysics (known as the Heisenberg Institute), the administrative building of the German Research Association (Deutsche Forschungsgemeinschaft) at Bad Godesberg, and the Germanisches Nationalmuseum at Nuremberg. In 1953, together with Döllgast and Kirsten, he began the rebuilding of the Bavarian State Library in Munich.

Ruf was responsible, together with Eiermann, for the German section of the Brussels World Exhibition (1956–58), and for the German Academy of Administrative Sciences (Hochschule für Verwaltungswissenschaften) at Speyer (1957–58), and the office building of the Berliner Handelsgesellschaft in Frankfurt-on-Main (1961–1965). In 1962 he was appointed to the planning committee fot the government office district in Bonn, and designed the living quarters and reception rooms of the Federal Chancellor in the gardens of Schaumburg Palace.

Ruf has been a member of the Berlin Academy of the Arts since 1955. His architecture, based on modern ideas and on careful thought given to the task in hand, is clear, simple and logical in style and method. This is the ideal which he endeavours to impart to his pupils.

Hans Purrmann

Hans Purrmann was born in 1880 at Speyer, where his father was in business as a painter. At thirteen, Hans became an apprentice painter and distemperer in his father's workshop, but at the same time took lessons in drawing and painting as a preparation for his later studies at the Karlsruhe College of Arts and Crafts, which he entered at the age of seventeen. His studies here, however, contributed little to his development as an artist, his talents being developed more by outside impressions and contact with like-minded friends. In the winter months, when things were quiet in his father's workshop, he began to study at the Academy in Munich, following in the footsteps of Klee and Kandinsky as a pupil of Stuck. The years that followed were hard ones, marked by disappointments and qualified successes; in the summer he would be at Speyer, painting shop signs and the like, in winter in Munich and Berlin.

In 1906 he moved to Paris, where he soon joined the circle of the Café du Dôme. His meeting with Matisse, with whom he maintained a close friendship in later years, was a turning-point in his life. It was at this time that he met his wife, the artist Mathilde Vollmoeller, sister of the writer Karl Vollmoeller. The flat in Paris into which they moved after their marriage soon contained a choice collection of contemporary art. At the outbreak of the First World War, the flat was commandeered, and the pictures confiscated; Purrmann never recovered any of them.

In 1916 Purrmann moved to Berlin, where a fruitful period of work and exchange of ideas with good friends followed, until he and his family were driven into exile in 1935 by the changed political conditions. Most of Purrmann's works that remained in Germany were confiscated and destroyed as "decadent" ("entartet"). He went to Florence, where he was given the honorary post of director of the Villa Romana. In 1943 his wife died, and the same year Purrmann was forced to leave Italy; he was invited by friends to come to Switzerland, and settled at Montagnola.

Otto Dix

Otto Dix was born at Untermhaus in Thuringia in 1891, and after serving as apprentice to a painter, studied at the Dresden College of Arts and Crafts. He was one of the founders of the 1919 Group of the Dresden Secession. During the 1920 s he lived in Berlin, and was closely connected with the Expressionist movement there. Decried as a "decadent artist", he went in 1936 to live at Hemmenhofen on Lake Constance. Jean Cassou has written of him: "Otto Dix belongs to the realist school of German Expressionism, which has nothing in common with the emotional, subjective or 'picturesque' school, which dates from a somewhat earlier period, from the beginnings of this prolific movement. By contrast, Dix belongs to the school in which the artist, in a primitive, elemental, and at first aimless frenzy, encounters reality and 'rends it', as an animal driven by the hunting instinct rends its prey... this frenzy discharges itself in the course of his work in huge canvases in which brazen reality is fused with the burlesque dissonances of the artist's conception. In Dix's works reality is transformed into never-ending satire."

Reinhold Nägele

"We want no doctor, no academic! We vote for a locksmith!" Thus wrote Justinus Kerner, poet and physician at Weinsberg, when, in 1848, a representative was to be elected to the National Assembly at Frankfurt, as Otto Rombach relates. This locksmith, who was the only artisan to be elected to the Paulskirche Parliament, was Reinhold Nägele's grandfather.

Nägele himself was born in 1884 at Murrhardt, in the fine old house known as 'The Angel', and spent his childhood at Murrhardt and Stuttgart. He began to paint in 1908, and describes himself as self-taught. Nägele, a sensitive and imaginative observer, found plenty of scope for his brush in the romantic little town in the Murrhardt Hills, with its roofs and gables, telegraph wires, the people in the street, at the cattle market, at the fair; but the cafes of the city, circuses, the political scene of his day, crowds, street riots, also stimulated his imagination. Heedless of contemporary trends in art, he continued on his lonely path, steering a course between the excesses of mannerism and surrealism with the sure step of a sleepwalker. As a young man, Theodor Heuss wrote about Nägele's work: "These pictures, although not particularly pious in theme, were painted with the devotion of a man for whom the important thing was not bold innovation, but careful and conscientious work." In 1933 Nägele had to go into exile, his wife being Jewish, and the family settled in New York. Many of the paintings which he left behind were burned during the war. After the war Theodor Heuss, now Minister of Education for Württemberg, asked Nägele to return to Germany to take up a chair at the Stuttgart College of Art. Nägele refused at the time, returning to Murrhardt only two years ago, after the death of his wife.

27

Hap Grieshaber

Grieshaber was born at Rot-an-der-Rot in 1909 and went to school at Nagold and Reutlingen. After attending classes of Ernst Schneidler, calligrapher, at Stuttgart, while simultaneously serving an apprenticeship in typesetting, he spent some years abroad: London, Paris, extensive travels in Egypt and, above all, Greece made deep impressions on the young artist. On his return to Reutlingen, having adopted the maxim "malgré tout", he became the moving spirit in a group of artists who, like himself, wanted to preserve their artistic integrity. In the "Third Reich" this inevitably meant resistance. The "Reutlinger Drucke" (Reutlingen Prints) bear witness against the evil spirit of the era. Grieshaber then devoted himself entirely to the woodcut. "Like the farmer with his plough, the gardener with his spade, and the butcher with his chopper", as he expresses it, "the wood-engraver with his knife is protected by the laws of his craft, which allow no undisciplined or irresponsible experimentation, but are a corrective of Nature." In 1951 Grieshaber became head of the Bernsteinschule, a small private art school at Sulz on the Neckar, and from 1955 until his resignation in 1960 he held a professorship at the College of Art in Karlsruhe. His spiritual home, however, has remained the Achalm, a hill near Reutlingen.

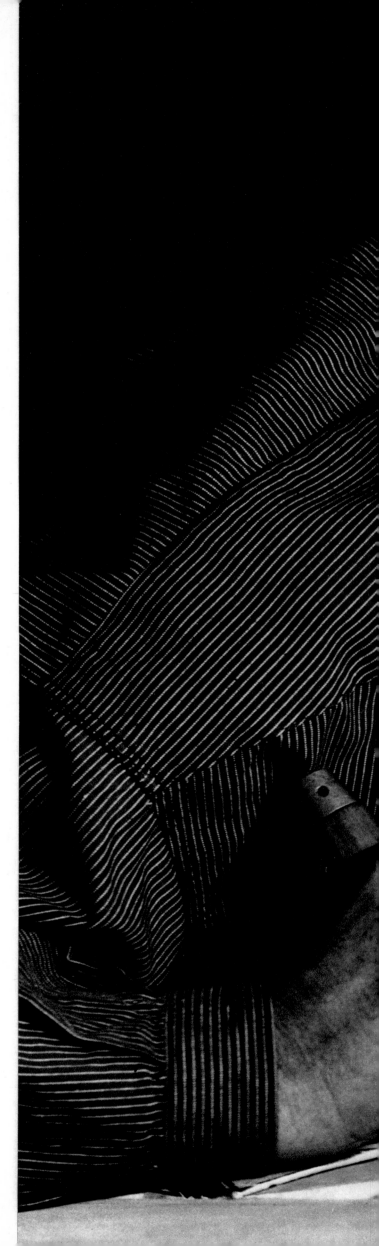

Fritz Winter

Fritz Winter has defined his standpoint as an artist in a letter as follows: "My work does not appear to reflect nature; appearances are deceptive, however, for it does, but in shapes and forms of my creating, not those of nature. I do not try to show what exists, but to reveal what is beyond what exists; for there is much more to be seen than we are able to see, and much more to be heard than we are able to hear, and there are many things beyond our own existence. What is important to me is that which is potential in us."

Winter was born at Altenbögge in Westphalia in 1905, and in 1927 became a student at the Bauhaus, where he was taught by Klee, Kandinsky and Schlemmer. He became close friends with Kirchner. In 1935 Winter moved to Diessen on the Ammersee. He was branded a "decadent artist", and forbidden to paint or to exhibit. In 1939 Winter was called up, and in 1945 taken prisoner by the Russians, not to be released until 1949, when he returned to live at Diessen. His work has been exhibited in numerous one-man shows in Europe and America, and he has been represented at all important national and international exhibitions. Winter has been awarded a number of prizes, for example at the Venice Biennale in 1950, the Sao Paulo Biennale in 1955, the Milan Triennale in 1954, and the Brussels World Exhibition in 1958. Since 1955 he has taught at the College of Art in Kassel.

Horst Antes

On the occasion of Antes's first exhibition in Berlin, Heinz Ohff wrote: "Horst Antes is the most successful of the young painters of today, at least in the German-speaking countries. At 28 he already ranks among the prominent in the world of art. His name is much bandied about, and his return to 'figurative' composition–which he, a pupil of Grieshaber, had never quite abandoned–is one of the most-discussed events of recent years. Artists of his own generation, especially those from the same stable–and Grieshaber's pupils are numerous–are tending to be compared with him, judged by his standards, or even declared outright to be his imitators…"

Antes was born in 1936 at Heppenheim an der Bergstrasse, in Rheinhessen; there he went to grammar school, taking his school-leaving examination in 1957, after which he went to study under Grieshaber at the Academy of Art in Karlsruhe. In 1959 he was awarded the Art Prize of the City of Hanover, and the Pankofer Prize in connection with the German Youth Art Competition; in 1960 the bursary of the Kulturkreis, in 1961 the Prix des Artistes de la IIe Biennale des jeunes artistes, Paris, in 1962 the Villa Romana Prize, Florence, and in 1963 a bursary of the Villa Massimo, Rome. At this time Hap Grieshaber wrote to his pupil in Rome: "I am not worried about your future. You set new standards by starting with a light touch, half hiding your startling themes in a tender grey, but then plunging into colour (I need have no qualms about showing your gouaches to my daughter). Your inspiration is plainly not quite of this world; the results are not coagulated or bogged down by time. You are not bound by any particular theme; the artist must be free to develop. You do not entirely discard personality, which nowadays is so much in jeopardy. He who loves à plein cœur–when things come from the very heart, as thea say in India–gives us deeper insight into things."

Gerhard Marcks

Gerhard Marcks grew up in Berlin, where he was born in 1889. His childhood paradise was the Berlin zoo; animals were his first friends and models, and it was a long time before his interest extended to human beings. The undisguised expressiveness of animals has never ceased to fascinate this eminent sculptor of the human form, and he confesses that it was from animals that he learned patience. He received his training in sculpture from Richard Scheibe in Berlin. From 1919 to 1925 he was in charge of the Dornburg pottery work-shop of the Weimar Bauhaus. From 1925 until 1933, when he was dismissed by the new regime, he was teacher and director at the College of Arts and Crafts at Halle-Giebichenstein. After the war, in 1946, he was appointed to a teaching post at the College of Art in Hamburg. In 1950 he moved to Cologne. Marcks is a member of the Berlin Academy of the Arts, and the Bavarian Academy of Fine Arts. He holds various awards, and is a member of the Order Pour le Mérite for Arts and Science. "Marcks has a masterly way of simply taking over shapes, or elements of form, from other times and cultures... this involves the capacity for adapting the remote and the exotic to his own needs... This gift places Marcks among the masters; for in the process he never abandons the firm foundation of his own attitude to art and life." (Günter Busch)

Otto Baum

Otto Baum was born in 1900 at Leonberg in Württemberg, began by becoming an apprentice motor mechanic, then served in the Navy during the First World War. He studied under Spiegel and Waldschmidt at the Academy in Stuttgart from 1924 to 1927 and from 1930 to 1933, after which he worked in Stuttgart as a freelance. As early as 1930 Paul Westheim drew attention to the young sculptor. Baum's first important work was commissioned by the architect Paul Bonatz, and included the reliefs for the firm of Hahn and Kolb, the Savings Bank at Stuttgart, and the reservoir dam at Neckar-Gerach.

When Baum's work was branded "decadent art" in 1933, he was forced to work in secret, and even to bury some of his larger works, for example the "Urmutter" (Universal Mother), which today stands in the parliament building at Stuttgart.

In 1946 Baum was appointed by Theodor Heuss, then Minister of Education for Württemberg, to a chair at the Academy in Stuttgart, where he taught the advanced sculpture class until 1965. Attention has been attracted especially by his "Elefantenmal" (Elephant Statue) in concrete at Zuffenhausen (1953), the concrete relief at the Stuttgart slaughter-house (1957), the sculpture "Das grosse Spiel" (The Great Game) for the University Hospital at Freiburg-im-Breisgau (1959), the "Mahnmal" (Memorial) at the Secondary Technical School in Stuttgart (1960), a two-sided wall relief, the 25-foot-high concrete sculpture "Schiffahrts-Symbol" (Shipping Symbol) at the pierhead at Deizisau (1963), and the 18-foot-high bronze in the Forum of the College of Education at Ludwigsburg (1965).

Karl Hartung

" 'We can feel that the new sculpture is on its way,' wrote D. H. Kahnweiler in 1915 in an essay on 'The Nature of Sculpture', influenced by Cubist ideas. 'There are abundant signs of it. What will it be like? Will it break through the surface of bodies and show us them from within, opened up? Most likely.' His prediction has come true. Hartung, who was born in 1908 in Hamburg, is one of the pioneers of this development. When, during the years from 1929 to 1932, he lived and worked in Paris, he did not yet recognize his predecessors in older artists like Archipenko and Brancusi. He was fascinated by the work of Maillol, by the discovery of 'poussé', of volume, of the 'beauty in tension' of still unfinished works by Despiau, which he saw in the making. From 1932 to 1933 he was in Florence, where he was struck by the way in which, in Donatello's works, 'the bones show through the flesh, the hardness within making itself visible through the softness outside' (here, perhaps, was the germ of inspiration which led to Hartung's 'Urgeäst' figures); and it was Etruscan art that first gave him the idea of a new approach to objective form through abstract shapes and symbols. He took this decisive step in 1935, when back in Hamburg, encouraged by Sauerlandt and his circle. Germany was now in the grip of a rigid artistic isolation; and Hartung, unable to continue his work except in secret, now discovered the kindred spirits of an older generation. His production at this time became known only at the end of the war, during which Hartung was called up, and later taken prisoner; it proved to be work bearing witness to a rapid development, as valid as any of its time, and calculated to dispel any fears of an eclipse of art in Germany. The fact that Hartung carried on his work in Berlin from 1936 onwards, and his work as a teacher at the Academy of Art (since 1951) and as president of the League of German Artists (as successor to Hofer), serve to indicate the attraction of, and influences emanating from, Berlin as a centre of art even today." (Walter Hess)

Bernhard Heiliger

Bernhard Heiliger first became acquainted with the art of sculpture in 1932 at the College of Arts and Crafts of his home town, Stettin. In 1938, at the age of 23, he went for the first time to Paris, where he was fascinated by the work of Maillol and Brancusi. His torsos dating from this period reveal his feeling for working with generous proportions. In the 1950s his torsos gradually became based less and less on the anatomical form of the human body and more and more on vegetable and organic shapes. This process of 'transformation' has become one of the basic principles of Heiliger's art. His participation in the international competition for the "Statue of an Unknown Political Prisoner" in 1952 inspired him with the theme of the tension between human or, in more general terms, organic form, and sharp, pointed bars. "Sculpture does not consist of playing with aesthetic shapes, but is concentrated vitality and spatial reality. It grows in space, feeling its way carefully, blossoms plant-like, or beats against it with great pulsations, or again floats through it, transcendent—becoming tangible and yet ever-changing poetry, consisting of crests and troughs, calm shapes and gaping abysses." Among Heiliger's most important works are the "Figurenbaum" (Tree of Figures) created for the World Exhibition in Brussels in 1958, the "Flammenzeichen" (Symbol of Flames) in the Ernst Reuter Platz in Berlin (1962/3), and a series of 15 reliefs for the Senate House at Bremen (1964/5); famous among his portraits are the busts of Ernst Reuter (1954) and Theodor Heuss (1960).
Bernhard Heiliger now lives in Berlin, where he teaches at the Academy of Art.

Arnold Bode

Arnold Bode holds a chair at the College of Art in Kassel, where he supervises a painting class. He became known far beyond the borders of Germany as the initiator and organizer of the first Documenta exhibition in 1955, and it is largely thanks to him that the most important international exhibition of art after the Venice Biennale now takes place at regular intervals on German soil, in Kassel— Documenta II in 1959, Documenta III in 1964. Bode is now chairman of the planning committee for Documenta IV, due in 1968.

Bode was born at Kassel in 1900. He studied at the College of Art in his home town from 1919 until 1925. In 1933 he went to Berlin to teach at the Handicraft Teachers' Training College in Berlin, but was dismissed the same April as "decadent". He was forbidden to exhibit, and supported himself and his family by designing interior decoration. The whole of his work was destroyed by bombing during the war. In 1945 he was released from internment as a prisoner of war by the Americans, and in 1947 was one of the founders ot the Kassel Academy of Crafts, which has now become the College of Art.

Heinrich Böll

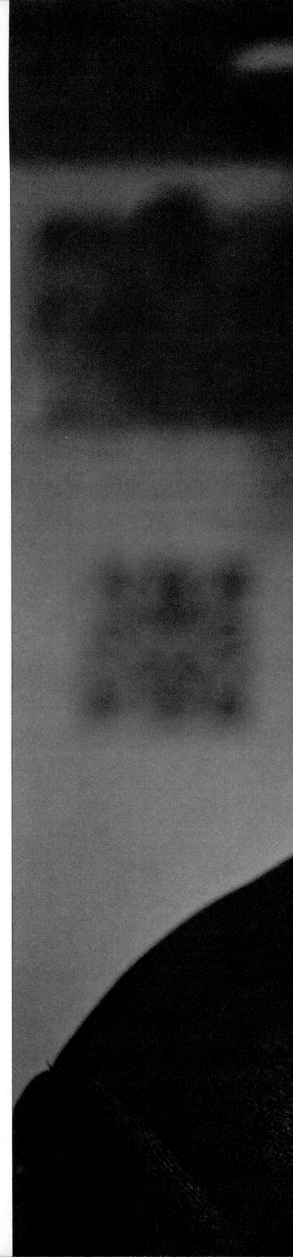

Heinrich Böll lives in Cologne, where he was born in 1917. He writes: "There are two Colognes which were my home; pre-war Cologne, between Raderthal and the Chlodwigplatz, between the Vorgebirgstrasse and the Rhine... the second Cologne, the ruined Cologne to which we returned in 1945, was different from the first, and has itself now vanished... The present Cologne is as remote from these others as Frankfurt from Stuttgart. ...Yet it is the first for many whose conscious lives are only now beginning." These words contain a hint of Böll's faculty for seeing his own experiences in the perspective of the great events of the times, for making them the experiences of others, of the many, of his characters. Böll is one of the few true storytellers of the present day; his first short story appeared in 1946. In 1951 he was awarded the prize of the '47 Group, in 1953 the Critics' Prize. Wolfgang Weyrauch has written about him: "We can feel the eternal wind of literary creativity blowing through Böll's stories, but with it mingle the whirlwinds that blow up from the public square and the open road, and the product is a literature of rebellion against blind convention, indolence and stupidity, a literature of analysis, telling the truth, interpreting it. It is a voice of reason."

Uwe Johnson

Uwe Johnson was born at Cammin in
Pomerania in 1934; his ancestors were
North German and Swedish farmers.
He studied German literature at Rostock
and Leipzig until 1956. In 1959 he
moved to West Berlin, where he
published his first novel, "Mutmassungen
über Jakob" (Speculations about Jakob).
In 1960 he was awarded the Fontane
Prize of the City of Berlin, and
Erhart Kästner declared at the time that
"his style was congruent with his
diagnosis of things". In 1962 he was
awarded the international publishers'
prize, Prix Formentor. Johnson's
theme is the division of Germany, which
has almost become "accepted reality".
His latest book, "Zwei Ansichten"
(Two Points of View), contains a double
biography and a two-fold description
of the city of Berlin. The Times
Literary Supplement commented on it as
follows: "Herr Johnson's prose has
an incisive, almost sullen, reticence in
which not a few Germans under forty
will recognize their own voices—
and silences."

Martin Walser

On being awarded the Hermann Hesse Prize in 1957, Martin Walser confessed: "A writer must really feel affection for all his characters, even the ones whom the reader feels to be unpleasant. It's always something of a love affair..." This gives us an agreeable insight into the workings of the mind of an author whose "sullenness derives from a positive attitude towards life", as the critic Marcel Reich-Ranicki has said. "His bitterness conceals subdued hope. Provocative he is, yes, but with a smirk... not a mere denouncer, but a moralist, and not an implacable or melancholy one, but a mild and indulgent one. His favourite tone is one of affable sarcasm." Walser was born in 1927 at Wasserburg on Lake Constance. He studied literature, philosophy and history at Tübingen, and took his doctor's degree in 1951 with a thesis on the works of Franz Kafka. Four years later he was awarded the prize of the '47 Group, and in 1962 the Gerhart Hauptmann Prize. Walser is one of the most-discussed of young German writers, with his novels "Ehen in Philippsburg" (The Gadarene Club) and "Halbzeit" (Half-time), and his plays "Eiche und Angora" (The Rabbit Race) and "Der schwarze Schwan" (The Black Swan).

Günter Grass

Günter Grass was born at Danzig
in 1927. He was wounded in the
Second World War at the age
of seventeen, taken prisoner by
the Americans, and released in
1945 with permission to settle in
the Rhineland. He tried his
hand at various trades, including
that of stonemason, and in 1949
began to study under Mages
and Pankok at the Düsseldorf
Academy of Art. In 1953 Grass
moved to Berlin and worked
under Karl Hartung. Gottfried
Benn recognized some of his
experiments in poetry as
showing talent, but advised the
young author to practise prose
writing. In 1955 Grass was
awarded a poetry prize, and
shortly afterwards was asked to
give a reading to the
'47 Group. In 1959 he
published his novel "Die
Blechtrommel" (The Tin Drum),
which achieved world-wide
success. "Gleisdreieck"
(Junction), "Katz und Maus"
(Cat and Mouse) and
"Hundejahre" (Dog Years)
followed.

50

Erich Maria Remarque

Erich Maria Remarque was born at Osnabrück in 1898; 1916 saw him as a soldier, 1919 a teacher, 1920 head of a monumental masonry business, journalist, critic, editor. In 1928 he wrote "Im Westen nichts Neues" (All Quiet on the Western Front). It was refused by S. Fischer, the publishers, on the grounds that it would not sell, as nobody wanted to read about the war any longer; it was published instead by the Propylæa publishing house in Berlin, and within six months had sold more than one million copies. It has been translated into 45 languages. It was banned in Italy until 1944, and in the Soviet Union for some years after the Second World War, as being too pacifist. Remarque's books were among those burnt in Germany in 1933. In 1936 he was deprived of his German citizenship, which he has never regained. In 1942 his sister was sentenced to death by the Nazi "People's High Court" and executed. Remarque now lives at Porto Ronco in Switzerland. All his books have been successful, and have been translated into more than twenty languages. His greatest success after "All Quiet on the Western Front" was "Arc de Triomphe" (Arch of Triumph).

Nelly Sachs

Nelly Sachs now lives in Stockholm. She was born in Berlin in 1891, the only child of factory owner William Sachs and his wife Margarethe, and spent her childhood in an elegant house in the Tiergarten district. Of her childhood she has said in a letter: "Above all there was the music-making of my father, who would improvise at the piano for hours on end, while I would dance to his playing, transported and with total abandon. When I was still quite small my dearest wish was to be a dancer. Even more than words, dancing was my way of expressing myself, my element; it is only owing to the harshness of the fate which befell me that I found my way to a different medium of expression, the poetic word." In her father's large library she early made the acquaintance of the myths and fairy tales of all times and peoples, and was particularly fascinated by the Romantics, and by books of Oriental wisdom. Her first poems were written at the age of 17, and many of her early writings were published in newspapers and magazines. Then came Hitler's rise to power. Nelly Sachs remained in Germany for seven years of fear and hardship, until the ageing Selma Lagerlöf succeeded in getting her and her elderly invalid mother to Sweden. The poems of this period appeared in the collection "In den Wohnungen des Todes" (In the Dwellings of Death); then came "Eli, ein Mysterienspiel vom Leiden Israels" (Eli, a Mystery Play of the Sufferings of Israel), and the poems "Sternverdunkelung" (Eclipse of the Stars). Her works are now available under the titles "Fahrt ins Staublose" and "Zeichen im Sand". In 1965 she was awarded the German Publishers' Peace Prize.

Ernst Jünger

"His most outstanding quality is the faculty of detachment; Jünger has the gift of a second self, which calmly and rationally observes and records the feelings and emotions of the first." Thus wrote Eugen Gottlob Winkler in 1936, shortly before his early suicide. There were many other alert and sceptical spirits of the generation that grew up between the wars who were fascinated by the hard, cold flame of Jünger's adventurous spirit, whether they venerated or opposed his ideas. His experiences in the "Steel Storm" of the war ("In Stahlgewittern"), the conjuring up of the "Staubdämonen" (Demons of the Dust), his vision of "The Worker", the dreams of a writer "To the Man in the Moon", his masterly evocations of the sight and feel of both Northern and Southern landscapes, owe their originality as reflections of the reality with which we are familiar to that detachment to which Winkler was referring.

Ernst Jünger was born at Heidelberg in 1895, and spent his childhood at Hanover as one of five children, of whom he is particularly close to his brother Friedrich Georg, his junior by three years. At school he was a dreamer and a voracious reader. Early on he conceived the desire to see the world on his own, and in 1913 ran away to join the French Foreign Legion, but his father succeeded in securing his return. At the outbreak of war in 1914 he volunteered for the army, and was sent to the Western front; during the war he was wounded fourteen times, and in 1918, by now a lieutenant, was decorated with the Order Pour le Mérite. For a time after the war he served in the Reichswehr, from which he obtained his discharge in 1923 to study science at Leipzig and Naples. In 1925 he moved to Berlin, where he lived as a free-lance writer, and married Gretha von Jeinsen. In 1933 Jünger left Berlin, declining an offer of membership of the new Academy of Writers. In the Second World War he joined the army as a captain. His eldest son Ernst was killed in action in Italy in 1944. Since 1950 Jünger has lived at Wilflingen, at the Southern edge of the Swabian Alb.

Boleslaw Barlog

Boleslaw Barlog is director of the Schiller Theatre, the Schlosspark Theatre and the Schiller Theatre's "Experimental Workshop" in Berlin, where he endeavours to maintain the high standard of company acting for which the Berlin stage of former decades was famous. He was born in 1906; from 1930 to 1933 he was, in his own words, "tea-boy, super and eventually assistant producer to Karl Heinz Martin and Heinz Hilpert at the old Volksbühne (People's Theatre) in the Bülowplatz." From 1937 to 1939 he was assistant producer, and from 1939 to 1945 producer, with the film companies Terra and Ufa, and was proud of the fact that during this time there was none of his films in which even a postman pronounced the words "Heil Hitler".

His most successful theatrical productions have been Shakespeare's "As you Like It", "The Taming of the Shrew", "A Midsummer Night's Dream" and "Much Ado About Nothing"; "The Time of Your Life" and "The Human Comedy" by William Saroyan; "The Devil's General" and "The Captain of Köpenick" by Carl Zuckmayer; "The Diary of Anne Frank" by Goodrich and Hackett; Chekhov's "Uncle Vanya" and "Three Sisters"; Büchner's "Leonce and Lena"; Lessing's "Minna von Barnhelm" and "Nathan the Wise"; Hauptmann's "Before Sunset", and Albee's "Who's afraid of Virginia Woolf?"

A music lover, Barlog has also produced operas: Puccini's "La Bohème" at the German Opera House in Berlin in 1963, Nicolai's "Merry Wives of Windsor" at the Hamburg State Opera, and Mozart's "Don Giovanni" at the National Theatre, Mannheim. He has defined his aim as follows: "If I am the worst producer in the theatres under my control, I shall consider these theatres well run." This sounds humble, but is proudly meant, as he himself says.

Wieland Wagner

Wieland Wagner, together with his brother Wolfgang, has been in charge of the Bayreuth Festival since 1949. He was born at Bayreuth in 1917, the son of Siegfried Wagner and his wife Winifred. His artistic talent showed itself clearly, and he studied painting, music and theatrical production largely on his own. He has never had any strictly professional stage training, but has relied on his own flair and hard work, with the advantage, as he sees it, that he avoided becoming stereotyped. Like his famous grandfather—of whom he says that, apart from family ties, he feels him to be as remote as Aeschylus, and, indeed, that it is only the distance in time that allows him to breathe freely in the presence of his genius—he is a fanatical champion of 'total theatre', that is, combining all the static and dynamic elements of a production in the true spirit of the work. He has freed his grandfather's work from the trammels of the 19th century, got at the essence of the works, and cleared away errors and misunderstandings that still find vent in biased judgments both positive and negative. With his original productions in the so-called 'New Bayreuth Style', he has succeeded in keeping Wagner's music alive and topical, and the most eloquent testimonial to his achievements is the readiness of a new and unprejudiced generation of visitors to the Festival to discover Wagner afresh.

It is, however, not only with Wagner that his work is concerned. Many theatres both at home and abroad have seen his productions of, for example, Gluck's "Orpheus", Beethoven's "Fidelio", Orff's "Antigonæ", and Berg's "Lulu" and "Wozzeck". He is particularly fond of Bach, Mozart, Ravel, Schönberg and Orff, and is interested in the history of art, comparative religion, and psychology.

Harry Buckwitz

Harry Buckwitz was born in 1904 in Munich, and studied drama under Arthur Kutscher. His stage career really began as an actor of old men's parts at the Munich Kammerspiele under Otto Falckenberg, and in Bochum under Saladin Schmitt—he played "nothing but greybeards", from Kreon in Grillparzer's "Medea" to Prospero in "The Tempest". In 1937 Buckwitz emigrated to East Africa, to try his luck as a hotelier at the foot of Mt. Kilimanjaro. The end of the Second World War was the beginning of a new life for him; he became director of the Munich Volkstheater, then of the Kammerspiele. "I rebuilt the ruined theatres, did administrating and producing", he writes. "But energy alone was not enough; a whole reputation had to be built up again from scratch." The Kammerspiele owed its post-war prestige to the pride that its team of outstanding actors, producers and stage designers took in belonging to this particular theatre. In 1951 Buckwitz became director of the Frankfurt municipal theatres, and from this time onwards has devoted his attention chiefly to the building-up of an ensemble and a repertoire. He has always stressed the cultural commitment of the theatre as the necessary foundation of his work; apart from this, he is convinced that the dramatist's words are more important than any artifices of interpretation.

His productions range from Shakespeare, Schiller and Lenz to Brecht, Frisch and Dürrenmatt.

Fritz Kortner

"A rebel, a revolutionary, a man of protest, impulsive and yet meditative, a master of all the tricks of the stage, and yet fired by intellectual ambition… a problematic actor and a portrayer of problematic characters", wrote Wolfgang Drews of Fritz Kortner on the occasion of his 70th birthday. He was born in Vienna in 1892, the son of a Jewish watchmaker. He developed a passion for the theatre, at first against his father's will; the first deep impression was made on him by the acting of Josef Kainz. After leaving school and the Academy of Dramatic Art, he was soon summoned by Max Reinhardt to Berlin. He acted in Vienna, Dresden, Hamburg, and, most of all, in Berlin, until his emigration to the U.S.A. via Switzerland and England with his wife and two children in 1938. His exile, and the terrible fate of many of his relatives, did not prevent him from returning, as early as 1949, to a Germany in ruins which he must always have thought of as his spiritual home. He now lives in Munich.

Karl Heinz Stroux

Karl Heinz Stroux began his career in 1927, at the age of nineteen, as an actor and producer at the Volksbühne and other theatres in Berlin, where he collaborated with Max Reinhardt, Jürgen Fehling and Karl Heinz Martin. In 1932 he staged the first performance in Germany of O'Neill's "All God's Chillun Got Wings", which already met with the disapproval of Nazist circles. In 1939 he was engaged by Gründgens at the German State Theatre. After the Second World War, Stroux was one of the first to bring back on to the German stage foreign plays which had been banned for the previous twelve years; in 1946, for example, Wilder's "The Skin of Our Teeth", "Antigone", etc. He played a leading part in the development of the Ruhr Festival. Stroux was chief producer at the Hebbel Theatre and the Schiller Theatre in Berlin and the Burgtheater in Vienna, and director of the theatres at Heidelberg, Darmstadt and Wiesbaden. His first production on taking over the direction of the Düsseldorf Playhouse in 1955 was symbolically, as it were, Calderon's "Gran Teatro del Mundo". He has said: "The sole task of theatrical art is to place itself, in all its tragic or comic variety, at the service of the dignity and aspirations of man, his freedom, and at the same time the obligations placed upon him by his existence in time in the world about and above him."

Elisabeth Bergner   Walter Richter

Elisabeth Bergner began her rise to fame after being engaged at the Deutsches Theater in Berlin by Alexander Moissi. She was born in Galicia in 1897, and spent her childhood and adolescence in Vienna, where she studied at the Conservatory. Her first engagement took her to Innsbruck; next came Zurich, and then the Kammerspiele in Munich, where she played opposite Moissi. After 1922 she acted mainly in Berlin, at the Barnowsky theatres, at the Deutsches Theater under Max Reinhardt, and at the State Theatre. The highlights of her film career were "Der träumende Mund" (The Dreaming Mouth) and "Ariane". She became a world-famous star, the idol of a generation, the frail charm of her voice and figure exercising an inimitable fascination. She scored great hits as Rosalind in "As You Like It", as Shaw's "Saint Joan", Schnitzler's "Fräulein Else", and Strindberg's "Miss Julie". In 1933 she was forced to emigrate to England, from where she went on to America; in these countries, too, she achieved great popularity. Since 1949 she has again appeared in Germany on a number of occasions, again proving her histrionic talent and power of suggestion in Rattigan's "The Deep Blue Sea", O'Neill's "Long Day's Journey into Night", and as the "Madwoman of Chaillot".

Walter Richter is a pupil of Ferdinand Gregori. After his first engagements, he acted under Heinz Hilpert in Berlin and Vienna. Since 1948 he has been a permanent member of the Zurich Playhouse company, but spends part of his working year in Germany, and regularly tours Switzerland, Germany, Austria and Belgium. Recently he played Captain Edgar in Strindberg's "Dance of Death", on the first German-language tour of Israel. His most important parts are the village judge Adam in Kleist's "The Broken Pitcher", the title rôle in "Drayman Henschel" by Hauptmann, Götz von Berlichingen, Captain Edgar, Büchner's Danton and Wozzeck, Meister Anton and Herod in Hebbel's plays, and Othello.

69

Ernst Deutsch

Ernst Deutsch was born in Prague in 1890, spending his childhood in the city in which writers like Rilke, Kafka and his friend Franz Werfel also lived. At the age of 24, at the request of Berthold Viertel, he went to Vienna, where he played his first parts at the Volkstheater (People's Theatre). Here he came into contact with Karl Kraus and Peter Altenberg, and became friends with Alfred Polgar. His first great success was in Dresden in 1916, in the title part of Walter Hasenclever's 'Expressionist' play "The Son". Not long afterwards he was summoned by Max Reinhardt to the Deutsches Theater in Berlin, at that time the focal point of new ideas and experimentation on the stage.

Deutsch, who used frequently to change his parts, and appear before the public in one new guise after another, has in recent years concentrated on his great classical roles: Nathan in Lessing's "Nathan the Wise", Shylock, Philipp II in Schiller's "Don Carlos", and Geheimrat Clausen in Hauptmann's "Before Sunset". His interpretations have left their mark on the German stage; he has helped to remove prejudice with his sensitive performances, of which his classic Nathan is a model. When he appeared on the stage in Berlin in 1951, for the first time since his return from exile, the audience rose to its feet to show its admiration for Deutsch by a long silence.

Elisabeth Flickenschildt

"She is one of those rare actresses", Siegfried Melchinger has written, "who act simultaneously with their senses, their nerves and their heads. She knows how to create a tension between the apparently voluntary human modes of expression and the apparently involuntary ones. She does not identify with herself; she is, quite simply, an actress all the time… Where the characters of a Flickenschildt appear on the stage, conventionality appears threadbare, and a cosy atmosphere mendacious."

Elisabeth Flickenschildt, the daughter of a sea-captain, was born in 1905 in Hamburg, where she attended grammar school; later she studied at the Academy of Dramatic Art in Munich. Here she had her first big part, under Falckenberg at the Kammerspiele in 1934, playing alongside Käthe Gold and Kurt Meisel. Then she went to Berlin, where she acted under the direction of Hilpert and Gründgens, and later to Düsseldorf and Hamburg. She has played a variety of parts both classical and modern, including Lady Macbeth, Queen Elizabeth in Schiller's "Mary Stuart", Frau Marthe in Goethe's "Faust", Lady Elizabeth in T. S. Eliot's "The Confidential Clerk", Clytemnestra, Atossa in "The Persians" of Aeschylus, and Mother Courage in Brecht's play.

We can gain some idea of the magical power of Elisabeth Flickenschildt's stage presence from Melchinger's account of her Lady Macbeth in Günther Rennert's Stuttgart production: "She was… surrounded by the strange aura that emanates from a woman who is urging a man on to murder, and herself becomes a murderess. Her tone of voice ranged from flattery to fury, from an 'unsexed' dreadfulness (as Shakespeare has it) to reluctant horror. I have never seen the sleep-walking scene so eerie; the gesture Shakespeare prescribes, 'thus washing her hands', haunts the memory, for one saw the very blood that she could smell… In the ghostly light of the flickering candles she appeared to transcend all earthly bounds."

Ernst Schröder

The actor and director
Ernst Schröder was born
in Westphalia in 1915.
He began his career
as assistant to Saladin
Schmitt. In 1938 he
joined the company of
the Schiller Theatre in
Berlin. From 1946 to
1948 he was in charge
of the Berlin Academy
of Dramatic Art.
Since 1958 Schröder has
also belonged to the
company of the Zurich
Playhouse. He plays the
great classical and
modern character parts.
In 1948 he published
the diary of an acting
school, under the title of
"Die Besessenen" (The
Possessed), in 1966
"Die Arbeit des Schau-
spielers" (The Actor's
Task).
"No actor before him",
writes Melchinger,
"has written so pro-
foundly about his art."

74

Antje Weisgerber

Antje Weisgerber was born at Königsberg in 1922; her father was a veterinary surgeon, her mother the dancer Lise Abt. She attended the Königin Luise Grammar School for Girls at Königsberg, and in 1939 was accepted for the State Academy of Drama attached to the then Prussian State Theatres in Berlin. Gustaf Gründgens was in charge, and her teachers included Herma Clement, Maria Koppenhöfer, and Walter Franck. At the age of 17 she appeared for the first time at the State Theatre in the Gendarmenmarkt, as Lucile in Büchner's "Death of Danton". In 1941 there followed a spell at the Munich Kammerspiele, where her first part was Laura in Heinrich Laube's play "Die Karlsschüler", with Horst Caspar as Schiller. She played Gretchen in Otto Falckenberg's production of Goethe's "Urfaust". Next she returned to the Berlin State Theatre, and in 1943 was engaged at the Burgtheater in Vienna until the theatres were closed in 1944.

She married Horst Caspar, and in 1944 her first child, Frank, was born, followed a year later by Renate. At the end of the war she returned to Berlin; in 1949 she went to Düsseldorf for the first time, at the request of Gründgens.

She took part in the first German contribution to the Edinburgh Festival, as Gretchen in Goethe's "Faust", together with Horst Caspar as Faust and Gründgens as Mephisto. On 27th December 1952, Horst Caspar died, and their son Frank a week later. In 1955 Antje Weisgerber followed Gründgens to Hamburg. In 1958 she married Reinhard Schilling. She played in "Faust" in New York in 1961, and in Venice in 1962, has taken part in the Salzburg Festival six times, and in 1965 won the Hersfeld Prize. Her most important parts include those of Juliet, Gretchen, Helen of Troy in "Faust", Donna-Proëza, Mary Stuart, and the title rôles in Schiller's "Maid of Orleans" and Lessing's "Minna von Barnhelm".

Boris Blacher

Boris Blacher was born at Nevkhvang in Manchuria in 1903, of Baltic parents, and had a restless childhood, with many changes of school, before the family moved to Irkutsk in Siberia in 1914. He learned to play the piano at an Italian convent school in Hankow. In 1917 the family fled from the revolution to Harbin, where many Russian exiles gathered, including a good many musicians. They formed an orchestra, whose conductor taught young Boris, giving him the task of orchestrating grand operas, of which only the piano scores were available; the result was such curiosities as Puccini's "Tosca" à la Tchaikovsky. Boris's father refused to allow him to study music, and sent him to Berlin to become an architect, but he was still strongly attracted by music. He found a teacher of composition in Friedrich Koch at the Academy of Music; as soon as his father heard of this, he cut off his allowance, so Boris kept himself alive by playing the harmonium in cinemas. It was at that time that he composed his first works, the first of which to be successfully performed was the "Konzertante Musik", conducted by Schuricht. At length, through the intervention of Karl Böhm, he obtained a teaching post at the Dresden Conservatory. Here he wrote the oratorio "The Grand Inquisitor", based on Dostoievsky's story, which, however, only had its first performance in Berlin in 1947, the same year in which he conducted his chamber opera "Romeo and Juliet". Blacher is particularly attracted by the ballet, perhaps because for him rhythm is the decisive factor in music; he has attempted to expand upon traditional rhythmical and metrical resources, and developed a technique of his own, which he used in his "Ornaments for Piano" and "Ornaments for Orchestra". He believes that music is developing away from the domination of harmony and counterpoint. Since 1947 Blacher has taught at the Berlin Academy of Music, and in 1953 he was appointed its director.

Carl Orff

Carl Orff's works include all the arts, of which music is only one component, albeit the decisive one. His musical system is centred on the sung and spoken word and he boldly exploits all the resources of the human voice. The instruments he uses are limited to giving tonal expression to the rhythmic element of his musical language. Carl Orff was born in Munich in 1895, attended grammar school there, and despite a period of study at the Academy of Music is really self-taught; coming from a family interested in all the arts he was already composing when only a child. In 1915 he became conductor at the Munich Kammerspiele, a chamber theatre directed by Falckenberg, where he came into close contact with the contemporary theatre. During this time Schönberg had the strongest musical influence on him. In 1924, together with Dorothee Günther, he founded the "Güntherschule". It was here that he discovered and developed his conception of the unity of music with movement and language that characterises his later work. Out of the work of this period grew Orff's "Schulwerk" ("Music for Children": musical education stimulating imagination through improvisation, using words in speech and song and simple percussion instruments).

"Carmina Burana" appeared in 1936. It belongs to the world of the theatre, a world that gives the greatest artistic scope for Orff's blend of words, music and gesture. Next came the fairy-tale operas "Der Mond" (The Moon) and "Die Kluge" (The Wise Woman), the Bavarian pieces "Die Bernauerin" (Agnes Bernauer) and "Astutuli", and the settings of Sophocles' "Antigone" and "Oedipus the King" in Hölderlin's translations.

Orff's new and quite individual conception of the essential relationship of language and music has made him an innovator in the field of musical drama; his works have received world-wide recognition. In 1961 a special Orff Institute was added to the Mozarteum in Salzburg. Orff is a member of the Order Pour le Mérite for Arts and Science.

Hans Werner Henze

"In my music the old forms gain a new importance, even where the modernity of its sound patterns completely, or almost completely, prevents them from appearing on the surface... they are to me... as refreshing as dreams, but incredibly difficult of access; nevertheless, the folly of attempting to get through to them seems to me the only thing worth living for." Hans Werner Henze was born at Gütersloh in 1926, the son of a primary-school teacher, began composing at the age of 12, and in 1942 went to study at the College of Music at Brunswick. In 1944 he was called up, and was subsequently taken prisoner by the British. It was not until 1946 that he was able to resume his studies, at the Institute of Church Music at Heidelberg; at the same time he was a pupil of Wolfgang Fortner. In 1948 he went to Constance as musical assistant to Heinz Hilpert, and from there to the Hesse State Theatre at Wiesbaden for two years, as conductor and artistic director of the ballet. In 1952 he settled in Italy, where he now lives and works. Since 1960 he has taught an advanced composition class at the Mozarteum in Salzburg, but lives in Rome.

His main field is the opera; among his operatic works are "König Hirsch", "Der Prinz von Homburg", "Der junge Lord" and "Die Bassariden".

Joseph Keilberth

Joseph Keilberth comes of a family of musicians. He was born at Karlsruhe in 1908, and studied the piano and cello in his home town. At the age of 17 he joined the Baden State Theatre at Karlsruhe as assistant conductor, and within ten years had worked his way up via the post of conductor to that of director of music. His profession later took him to Prague, Dresden, Berlin, Hamburg and Munich. He is now director of music at the Bavarian State Opera, and chief conductor of the Bamberg Symphony Orchestra. For him, technical mastery of a work goes without saying, but the essential thing is the interpretation; he holds virtuosity to be desirable, but sensitivity to the basic message of great music to be more important. He believes that a conductor should not specialize, but should have a command of the whole repertoire, not only of concert, but also of operatic music. His favourite score—the one that happens at any time to be to hand.

Eugen Jochum

Eugen Jochum was born at Babenhausen, near Augsburg, in 1902. His father was a schoolmaster, who ran the church choir and the local band, and conducted the orchestra at the little theatre there. By the age of five, Eugen was able to play the big drum, and pull the organ stops for his 80-year-old grandfather at church on Sundays. At nine, he used to help out as organist at the churches in nearby villages. In 1914 he went to the grammar school at Augsburg, and at the same time studied at the local College of Music. He took his school-leaving examination in 1922, during the period of inflation, and his father could not afford to pay for his musical studies; luckily, help was forthcoming from an uncle in America, who volunteered to pay for Jochum's training. He thus went to the Academy of Music in Munich, where his teachers were Joseph Haas, v. Waltershausen and Siegmund v. Hausegger, who discovered the talent of the budding conductor and introduced him, in particular, to the works of Anton Bruckner. A concert at which he conducted Bruckner's Seventh Symphony in 1925 made the young Jochum famous overnight. He was offered an appointment as conductor at Kiel, frequently conducted at Lübeck, and used to go to Hamburg to attend the concerts of Karl Muck and Wilhelm Furtwängler, whom he much admired. In 1929, on Furtwängler's recommendation, he went to the National Theatre at Mannheim, and then in 1932 to Berlin, which he soon left again, out of antipathy to the new regime, to take over the Hamburg Opera and Philharmonic Orchestra. He remained in Hamburg for sixteen years before moving in 1949 to Munich, where he built up the Bavarian Radio Orchestra.

In 1959 Jochum became the permanent guest conductor of the Concertgebouw Orchestra, Amsterdam, with which he toured the U.S.A. in 1961 and Japan in 1962. He has also toured with the Berlin Philharmonic Orchestra. He regularly conducts opera and philharmonic concerts in the main cities of Europe.

Hans Richter-Haaser

Hans Richter-Haaser was born at Dresden in 1912. From his mother, who came of a musical family, he inherited his talent, and from his father a feeling for proportion. His step-father, Bruno Haaser, arranged for his musical training at the Schneider Academy of Music, which, together with Fritz Busch, the Staatskapelle Orchestra, the Opera, the Philharmonic Orchestra and, not least, a succession of great soloists, gave him his most powerful early impressions. He won the Bechstein Prize, conducted choirs and orchestras, composed, taught and played chamber music. The Second World War deprived him of seven valuable years of development. His friends, in particular Ludwig Hoelscher, with whom he frequently gave concerts, prophesied his success, and were proved right. Richter-Haaser was appointed to teach at the North-West German Academy of Music, Detmold, but in 1955 gained an international reputation after playing with Paul van Kempen at Hilversum, and has since travelled all over the world, being much in demand for his renderings of Beethoven and Brahms. He likes playing Mozart and Schubert best. He has been to Paris and New York with the Berlin Philharmonic Orchestra, under Herbert von Karajan. Richter-Haaser is fond of reading and mountain walking, and collects minerals and fossils.

Ludwig Hoelscher

Ludwig Hoelscher's virtuosity has developed from his absolute self-discipline; he has won world fame with his playing. His performances of Bach and Beethoven are regarded as being as authentic as his interpretations of contemporary music. A number of works which have gone down in modern musical history owe their existence directly or indirectly to him. Works for the cello have been dedicated to him by Hans Pfitzner and other composers; Hoelscher has been responsible for the first performances of concertos by Ernst Krenek, Hans Werner Henze, Wolfgang Fortner, Karl Höller, Harald Genzmer, Heinrich Sutermeister and others, and for the first performances in Europe of a number of works by Paul Hindemith. He has travelled almost all over the world with the great conductors, orchestras and intrumentalists of our time as the leading German exponent of his instrument.

Hoelscher was born at Solingen in 1907, and grew up in a highly musical family. He was taught by Hugo Becker, Julius Klengel and Wilhelm Lamping, and in Berlin in 1930 won the Mendelssohn Prize, the highest award for students of music. His career as a soloist began in 1932, when he was discovered by Elly Ney, who asked him and Wilhelm Stross to join her to form the Elly Ney Trio, which soon acquired a high reputation throughout Europe. At the age of 29 he was appointed to a chair at the State Academy of Music in Berlin, since when he has regarded his teaching commitments, which have recently taken him to Salzburg and Stuttgart, as highly important.

Dietrich Fischer-Dieskau

The boyhood dreams of Dietrich Fischer-Dieskau—of becoming either an engine-driver or President of Germany—in time gave way to ambitions more in keeping with his pronounced musical talent, the question now being whether he was to become a conductor or a heroic tenor. In fact he became neither. He was born in Berlin in 1925, and grew up in musical surroundings, receiving his first lessons from his mother. Later he became a pupil of the great contralto Emmy Leisner, with whom he maintained admiring and grateful contact until her death. At the Academy of Music he was taught singing by Hermann Weissenborn, but after only one term his studies were interrupted by the war. As a prisoner of war, Fischer-Dieskau organized lieder recitals, and produced the operetta "Der Vetter aus Dingsda" in the camp; his career thus began behind barbed wire.

After the war he settled for a time at Freiburg, where he married, but soon returned to Berlin to continue his studies under Weissenborn. The recordings he made for RIAS of the "Winter Journey" and all of Bach's cantatas brought the young baritone immediate fame. Heinz Tietjen offered him an engagement at the Berlin Municipal Opera. In 1954 Wieland Wagner asked him for the first time to take part in the Bayreuth Festival, where he sang the part of Wolfram. Other important operatic rôles which he has sung include those of Mozart's Don Giovanni, Jochanaan in Strauss's "Salome", Alban Berg's Wozzeck, Hindemith's Mathis, and Mittenhofer in Henze's "Elegy for Young Lovers". He is a regular performer at musical festivals at home and abroad. Fischer-Dieskau's rapid rise to fame has been aided by the phenomenal sales of his gramophone recordings. He has made lieder his special field; his accompanists include Gerald Moore, Jörg Demus and Günter Weissenborn. He keeps his engagement list, normally full to overflowing, empty in June, which he spends at home with his family, busy with his collections and the puppet theatre which he is building for his sons.

Rudolf Augstein

Rudolf Augstein, the publisher and editor-in-chief of "Der Spiegel", was born at Hanover in 1923. At the age of twenty he found himself on the Russian front as an artillery observer; in 1945, by now a lieutenant, he was taken prisoner by the Americans. After his release, he abandoned his original intention of studying German literature, and worked on the "Hannoversches Nachrichtenblatt", a newspaper licensed by the British military government. In 1946 appeared "Diese Woche", a news magazine modelled on its English counterparts and still controlled by British press officers, in which Augstein was responsible for the coverage of German domestic affairs; he caused a stir by the publication of a letter from Victor Gollancz in the very first edition. On 4th January 1947, the paper's title was changed to "Der Spiegel", a name now familiar both inside and outside Germany.

The forthright and provocative style of "Der Spiegel" attracted readers from the outset. Augstein, who belonged for a time to the Free Democratie Party, now avoids any party slant in his leaders. "Der Spiegel" has sometimes been reproached with the fact that it avoids a clear political commitment; it certainly sees itself as being committed to tracking down and pouncing upon abuses of all kinds in society, the economy and the state, and not infrequently contributes to their alleviation. Augstein and his staff are helped in carrying out this self-imposed task by a sharp nose for controversial news, and a unique set of archives.

Countess Dönhoff

Marion Dönhoff comes from a family which in 1330 left Westphalia to go East, settling in the area between the Vistula and the Dvina, partly in Latvia, partly in East Prussia. During the following six centuries the Dönhoffs shared the changing fortunes of that part of Europe. There were times at which their name went down as frequently and momentously in Polish history as it did later in the annals of Prussia.

Countess Dönhoff was born in 1909 at Friedrichstein in East Prussia. After finishing school at Potsdam, she travelled extensively in Europe, America, and Africa, and eventually began the study of economics in Frankfurt-on-Main. When Hitler came to power in 1933, she moved to Basle, Switzerland, where, in 1935, she took her doctor's degree in economics. A year later she went to Friedrichstein to be trained in the administration of the family estates, which she took over in 1939. When the advancing Russian army reached East Prussia in January 1945, Marion Dönhoff found herself one of the many millions of refugees trekking westwards. She described this experience in her book "Namen, die keiner mehr nennt" (Names that are not mentioned any more). Chance, which at that time ruled the lives of most people, took her in the spring of 1946 to Hamburg, where she joined the staff of the newly founded weekly "Die Zeit", whose political editor she has been since 1955.

Will Grohmann

Will Grohmann came to be interested in modern art by way of that of ancient and prehistoric times. "This seems to me quite logical", he writes, "and I still think that present-day painting and sculpture are closer to the discoveries of non-classical archaeology than to the tradition of European art since the Middle Ages."

Grohmann was born at Bautzen in 1887; when he was four his family moved to Dresden, where he attended the Holy Cross Grammar School. He later studied oriental languages, in particular Sanskrit under Ernst Windisch at Leipzig. After his doctor's degree he devoted himself wholly to art.

His first love was the work of Ernst Ludwig Kirchner, a volume of whose drawings he edited in 1925. A year later followed his book on Kirchner, which was published by Kurt Wolff. At the same time he was fascinated by the work of Klee and Kandinsky. After the First World War Grohmann worked on the Thieme and Becker Encyclopaedia of Artists and the art review "Cicerone". He lived in Dresden where exhibitions of the Bauhaus painters Kandinsky, Klee, Schlemmer and Moholy-Nagy were held in galleries and private collections. In 1933 Grohmann was dismissed. Of the years that followed he writes: "... until the collapse of the 'Third Reich' I busied myself with archaeological matters, especially the art of the migratory peoples."

In 1947 he moved to Berlin, where he was appointed to a chair of history of art at the Academy of Arts a year later. Here he has been able to write the comprehensive monographs on Klee and Kandinsky, discussed in detail with the painters themselves, which had been planned for the 1930s. Among Grohmann's other publications, his work on Henry Moore deserves especial mention.

Joachim Kaiser

The son of a doctor, Joachim Kaiser was born at Milken in East Prussia in 1928. He began his schooling at Tilsit, but was forced by the events of the war to change frequently, attending grammar school at Tilsit, Elbing, Templin and Hamburg. He studied German literature, music and philosophy at Göttingen University from 1948 to 1951, then until 1954 in Frankfurt, where he was also a free-lance writer, and later worked for the Hessischer Rundfunk (Hesse Radio). He completed his doctoral thesis, on the dramatic style of Grill-parzer, at Tübingen in 1957, under Klaus Ziegler.

Since 1959 Kaiser has been dramatic, musical and literary editor of the Süddeutsche Zeitung in Munich. In 1965 he published a "Theatre Diary" and "Great Pianists of Our Time".

Adolf Butenandt

Adolf Butenandt was born at Bremerhaven-Lehe in 1903, studied chemistry and biology at Marburg and Göttingen, took his doctor's degree under Adolf Windaus in 1927, and, four years later, qualified as a university teacher, habilitating in organic and biological chemistry. From 1933 to 1936 he held a chair at the Institute of Technology at Danzig, then became director of the Kaiser Wilhelm Institute for Biochemistry in Berlin-Dahlem. In 1939 he was awarded the Nobel Prize for Chemistry for his research into the isolation, identification and synthesis of sex hormones. When the institutes were moved from Berlin to escape the bombing towards the end of the war, he went to Tübingen, where shortly afterwards he took over the chair of physiological chemistry. In 1956 the Institute, which since 1949 had borne the title of Max Planck Institute for Biochemistry, moved with its director to Munich, where Butenandt also continued his teaching.

Besides his teaching and research, Butenandt devotes time to numerous scientific and intellectual causes of public interest. He is one of the scholars who developed the present German Research Association (Deutsche Forschungsgemeinschaft) from the former German Research Concil (Deutscher Forschungsrat) and the Emergency Association of German Science (Notgemeinschaft der Deutschen Wissenschaft), and was a member of the Federal Commission for Educational Affairs.

In 1960 Butenandt took over the office of President of the Max Planck Society from Otto Hahn. In 1962 he became a member of the Order Pour le Mérite for Arts and Science.

Werner Heisenberg

Werner Heisenberg was born in Würzburg in 1901, and grew up in Munich, where his father was professor of Middle and Modern Greek (Byzantine art). After studying at the universities of Munich and Göttingen, he took his doctor's degree in Munich under Arnold Sommerfeld in 1923, and then became assistant to Max Born at Göttingen. After becoming a lecturer there, he was awarded a Rockefeller fellowship, and later worked as lecturer under Niels Bohr in Copenhagen. In 1927, the year of his discovery of the "uncertainty principle", Heisenberg was appointed to the chair of theoretical physics at Leipzig. In 1933 he received the Nobel Prize for Physics. Since 1941 he has been director of the Kaiser Wilhelm (later Max Planck) Institute for Physics, which until the end of the war was in Berlin, then in Göttingen, and since 1958 in Munich.

For several years he was chairman of the Scientific Policy Committee of the International Institute of Nuclear Physics in Geneva; since 1953 he has been president of the Alexander von Humboldt Foundation.

Heisenberg is a member of the Order Pour le Mérite for Arts and Science. In recent years his work has been concerned mainly with the unified theory of elementary particles, with which he hopes to gain a better understanding of the nature of matter.

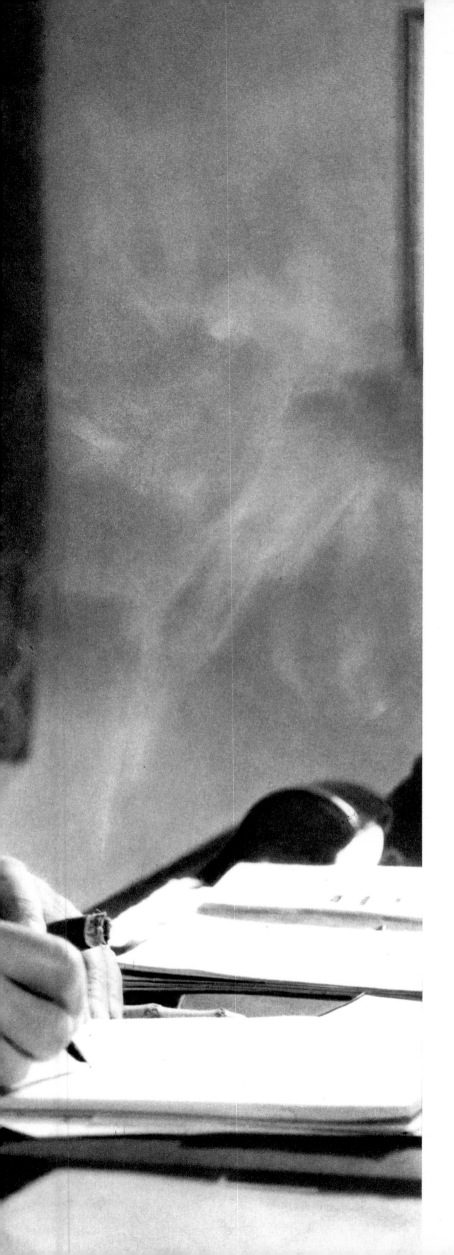

Otto Hahn

Otto Hahn was born in 1879 in the Bockgasse on the Liebfrauenberg in Frankfurt-on-Main, where his father had developed Schön's, the firm of glaziers, into an undertaking of considerable importance. It was his father's wish that Otto should become an architect but, as he says, "I could, I am afraid, hardly have been less suited for this profession". He began his studies of chemistry in 1897, at the universities of Marburg and Munich. In 1901 he took his doctor's degree at Marburg, and became assistant to Zincke at the Institute of Chemistry there. In 1904 he went to University College, London, to work under Sir William Ramsay, and spent part of the following year under Ernest Rutherford at the Institute of Physics at McGill University, Montreal. In 1907 he habilitated in chemistry under Emil Fischer in Berlin; the same year he met Lise Meitner, with whom he was to collaborate for over 30 years. In 1912 he became a member of the newly founded Kaiser Wilhelm Institute for Chemistry at Berlin-Dahlem, of which he was director from 1928 until 1945. From 1946 to 1960 he was president of the Max Planck Society. He received the Nobel Prize in 1944 for his discoveries in the field of radiochemistry.

Pascual Jordan

Pascual Jordan was born at Hanover in 1902, the son of Professor E. Jordan, the painter; here he began his studies of physics, mathematics and zoology and continued them at Göttingen. His teachers included Max Born, J. Franck, R. Courant, D. Hilbert and A. Kühn. Together with Born and Heisenberg, he developed the foundations of quantum mechanics and quantum electrodynamics. In 1927 he went to Copenhagen for a year to work under Niels Bohr. In 1929 he was appointed to the chair of theoretical physics at Rostock, then went to Berlin in 1944 as the successor of Max von Laue, and since 1947 has taught in Hamburg.

About his work he writes: "I was always attracted by research problems which were connected with basic questions of philosophy or epistemology. My student years were marked by the seemingly insuperable difficulties encountered by physicists in their early researches into quantum and atomic phenomena… Schrödinger's 'wave mechanics' had provided a new approach to the secret of quantum physics, apart from the 'quantum mechanics' developed by Heisenberg, Born and myself; later on my own research, together with Heisenberg's and Bohr's conceptions of the 'uncertainty principle' and 'complementarity', finally completed the picture of '20th-century physics', in which the fact that the principle of causality was weakened or rendered largely obsolete is only a symptom of the superseding of older ideas."

Jordan's work in biophysics strives to prove that statistical "acausality" also plays an important part in biology, and is in fact the distinguishing feature of organic, as compared to inorganic, matter.

Carl Friedrich v. Weizsäcker

Carl Friedrich v. Weizsäcker was born at Kiel in 1912. As he grew up he found himself, by reason of family tradition, poised between three spheres of life and thought: theology, science and politics. He intended to begin with the study of philosophy, but changed to physics on the advice of Werner Heisenberg. His insight into the historical development of physics and problems connected with it has shaped his whole thinking. Thus, from the first, he has seen the problems of physics in the light of the interaction of the twofold tradition of the humanities and the sciences. In this he is greatly indebted to his teacher Niels Bohr.

Weizsäcker habilitated in 1936, and was appointed to a lectureship at the University of Berlin. In time he passed from the study of the concrete sciences to more rigorous discipline, the science of knowledge, and in 1957 took over the chair of philosophy at Hamburg University. His thinking today is on a level where quantum physics, epistemology and analysis of the world of politics blend to form a homogeneous whole.

In 1961 Weizsäcker became a member of the Order Pour le Mérite for Arts and Science, and in 1963 was awarded the German Publishers' Peace Prize.

Max Born

Max Born grew up in Breslau, where he was born in 1882, in an intellectual home atmosphere with a marked scientific bias. He lost his mother at an early age; his father, a distinguished biologist, too, died before the young man had chosen his future subject of study. He followed his father's advice not to specialize too soon, and began with the study of astronomy, but soon turned to mathematics. After a number of semesters at the universities of Breslau, Heidelberg and Zurich, Born went to Göttingen, where Klein, Hilbert and Minkowski were teaching. In 1906 he won the faculty prize, and took his doctor's degree the following year. It was during his studies of experimental physics at Breslau that he learned of Einstein's work on the theory of relativity, dating from the previous year, which inspired him to research of his own in this field; then he was asked by Minkowski to return to Göttingen, where he habilitated in 1909. The theory of the specific heat of solids developed by Einstein was a pointer for Born to his main fields of quantum theory and crystal lattice, in which he worked at first in collaboration with Theodor v. Kármán. During the First World War there began a close friendship between Born and Einstein, which lasted until the latter's death.

In 1921 Born was called to a chair at Göttingen where, together with his pupils Heisenberg and Jordan, he worked out the theoretical basis of the new conception of physics, quantum mechanics. In 1933 Born and his family were forced to emigrate; he went to England, where he founded a school of theoretical physics. He returned to Germany at the age of seventy. In 1954, in recognition of his work on quantum mechanics, Born was awarded the Nobel Prize for Physics. The question which has occupied him most in recent years is whether, and how, the self-destruction of our civilisation by an atomic war can be avoided.

Feodor Lynen

Feodor Lynen is Professor of Biochemistry at the University of Munich. He was born in Munich in 1911, studied chemistry there, and in 1937 took his doctor's degree under Heinrich Wieland, who had been awarded the Nobel Prize for Chemistry in 1927, and who introduced him to dynamic biochemistry. Lynen remained faithful to his home university where, after his habilitation, he was appointed lecturer in 1942, and professor in 1953. One year later, at the recommendation of Otto Warburg and Otto Hahn, who was then president of the Max Planck Society, Lynen also became director of the Max Planck Institute for Cell Chemistry, which was set up especially for him, providing excellent facilities for his research. His work is mainly concerned with the chemical details of metabolic processes in living cells, and the mechanisms of the regulation of metabolism.

In 1964 Lynen was awarded the Nobel Prize for Physiology or Medicine.

Gerhard Schramm

Gerhard Schramm was born in 1910 in Yokohama. He studied at the universities of Munich and Göttingen and, after taking his doctor's degree under Professor Adolf Butenandt, began his academic career as an assistant in Danzig and at the Kaiser Wilhelm Institute for Biochemistry in Berlin-Dahlem. In 1952 Schramm became a member of the Scientific Council of the Max Planck Society. Since 1954 he has been director of the biochemical section of the Max Planck Institute for Virus Research at Tübingen, at the same time holding a chair at the university there. His special fields are molecular biology and virus research, particularly the latter. He has published numerous papers in learned periodicals on proteins and nucleic acids, together with books on "Die Biochemie der Viren" (The Biochemistry of Viruses) and "Belebte Materie" (Enlivened Matter).

Rudolf Mössbauer

Rudolf Mössbauer, who was born in Munich in 1929, studied physics at the Institute of Technology there; from 1955 to 1958 he carried out a number of research projects at the Institute of Physics at the Max Planck Institute for Medical Research at Heidelberg, in the course of which the first experimental observation of recoil-free nuclear resonant absorption was made. In 1961 Mössbauer was appointed professor at the California Institute of Technology at Pasadena, U.S.A., and the same year was awarded the Nobel Prize for Physics. Three years later he accepted an appointment to a chair of physics at the Munich Institute of Technology, the departmental system in this university being introduced there at the same time, for the first time in a German university. He still spends three months of each year at the California Institute of Technology at Pasadena.

Since 1953 Mössbauer's main field of research has been the study of the interaction of gamma radiation and matter. His work has led to the discovery of recoil-free nuclear resonant absorption (known as the Mössbauer effect) and its theoretical interpretation. In recent years he has applied the methods which he has developed to the investigation of problems of nuclear physics and solid state physics.

Otto Warburg

Otto Warburg was born at Freiburg in 1883. He studied chemistry in Berlin under Emil Fischer, thermodynamics under Walter Nernst, physics and photochemistry under his father, who was president of the State Institute for Physics and Technology, and later medicine under Ludolf Krehl. During the First World War he fought as a cavalry officer in Russia. In 1930 he was appointed director of the Kaiser Wilhelm Institute for Cell Physiology at Berlin-Dahlem. In 1931 Warburg received the Nobel Prize for Physiology and Medicine for the discovery of the chemical reaction by which oxygen reacts in the organic world. Respiration and fermentation, and the metabolism of normal and tumour cells, have remained Warburg's special fields until today. In 1944 the Stockholm Committee voted to award Warburg the Nobel Prize for the second time, for the discovery of the yellow enzymes and the hydrogen transfer by nicotinamide, but this was prevented by the political situation. Apart from himself three of his pupils have also been awarded the Nobel Prize, a unique record. In 1952 Otto Warburg became a member of the Order Pour le Mérite for Arts and Science.

Friedrich Förster

Friedrich Förster, the son of a parson, was born in 1908 at Hundisberg, near Magdeburg, and studied physics at Göttingen, taking his doctor's degree in 1932. He began his career as assistant to Arnold Eucken, then worked under Köster at the newly-founded Kaiser Wilhelm Institute for Metal Research at Stuttgart. His main field was the application of physical and electronic techniques to problems of metal research and testing. In 1948 Förster founded a research and production centre of his own at Reutlingen. From 1960 onwards he contributed to the American space programme, constructing the magnetic sensors for the 'Mariner' series. He has published numerous papers on physical measurement of magnetism and non-destructive testing of metallic material. In 1957 Förster received from the American Society for Nondestructive Testing the Alfred Victor DeForest Award for establishing the experimental and theoretical foundations of electromagnetic measurements.

125

Karl Heinrich Bauer

Karl Heinrich Bauer was born at Schwärzdorf in Upper Franconia in 1890, attended grammar school at Bamberg, and studied medicine at Erlangen, Heidelberg, Munich and Würzburg. During the First World War he was a medical officer with the infantry for 3 years. In November 1918 he began his academic career under Ludwig Aschoff at the Pathological Institute of Freiburg University. In 1919 he began his surgical training at Göttingen, under R. Stich. In 1932 he succeeded Küttner as professor of surgery and director of the surgical clinic at Breslau University, where he remained for ten years. In 1943 he took over Martin Kirschner's chair at Heidelberg. In 1945 Bauer became the first freely elected Vice-Chancellor (Rektor) of Heidelberg University.

Bauer's life's work in medical therapy has centred round cancer research. He is an indefatigable fighter for the prevention of cancer which, on the basis of a lifetime of research, he does not regard as an inescapable ill; he has continually urged state action in the struggle for the reduction of possible external causes of cancer, such as exhaust gases and the chemical pollution of water. Bauer is the initiator and one of the founders of the first German Cancer Research Centre at Heidelberg, and endowment trustee of the German Cancer Research Foundation. He is an honorary member of numerous learned associations, an honorary member of several scientific academies, and holder of the Henri Dunant Medal and of the Ernst von Bergmann Memorial Medal.

Hans-Erhard Bock

Hans-Erhard Bock was born at Waltershausen (Thuringia) in 1903, the son of a grammar school teacher. During the First World War he made up his mind to become a general practitioner. From 1922 to 1927 he received his medical training at the universities of Marburg, Munich, Jena, Bonn, and Hamburg. During this time he was influenced most by the lectures of F. v. Müller, Leblanc, and H. Schottmüller. As a postgraduate at St. Georg's Hospital in Hamburg from 1927 to 1933 he did research work under the pathologist Wohlwill, the pharmacologist Bornstein, and the neurologist Pette. He also worked under Hegler in the medical department. In 1933 he went to Frankfurt to join the team of F. Volhard, who promoted his scientific career most actively. In 1935 Bock qualified as a university teacher (Habilitation). Then he became associate professor under Friedrich Koch who had also been a member of Volhard's team (Tübingen 1938–1942 and Berlin 1942). During the Second World War he served as a medical consultant in Italy. In 1945 he returned to Tübingen University Medical Hospital under Bennhold as associate professor (Oberarzt). His chief scientific interests have always been hematological disorders and drug induced agranulocytosis, as well as chemotherapy. In 1949 he became director of Marburg University Medical Hospital. During the following thirteen years he formed a very efficient team of scientists who worked on clinical hematology, nephrology, hepatology, and cardiology. In 1953 he became Dean of the Medical Faculty, and in 1960 Vice-Chancellor (Rektor) of Marburg University. In 1962 he succeeded Bennhold as director of Tübingen University Medical Hospital. During all these years he has published numerous fundamental papers mainly on hematological disorders, angiopathies, drug therapy and side effects, allergy and chemotherapy of malignant diseases. He is co-editor of the manual "Klinik der Gegenwart". Bock believes in the efficacy of physical exercise which he recommends to people of all ages as an "antidote" to the progressive passivity of modern life.

Ernst Derra

Ernst Derra, the son of the sculptor Ernst Derra, was born at Passau in 1901. He studied medicine at Munich, Heidelberg and Vienna, and took his doctor's degree at Leipzig in 1927. After several years as an assistant at the university medical clinic at Leipzig and at the university surgical clinic at Bonn, he was appointed to a lectureship at Bonn University. Since 1946 Derra has been professor of surgery, and director of the surgical clinic of the Medical Academy, at Düsseldorf. His special field is thoracic surgery, with special emphasis on cardio-vascular surgery. His publications up to 1946 cover certain experimental studies, together with work on various problems of classical surgery and anaesthetics; since 1947 mainly problems of thoracic surgery. Of 195 papers to date, 90 are concerned with questions relating to, and developments in, the surgery of the heart and its large vessels. Derra is a member of numerous surgical associations both at home and abroad, an honorary member of many international learned societies, and president of several German and other European specialist associations. He holds several high awards for his achievements in the field of cardiac surgery. His lecture tours have taken him round the world.

Ludwig Heilmeyer

Ludwig Heilmeyer was born in Munich in 1899. He was strongly influenced by the world of his father, an art critic, so that he early conceived the ambition to study the history of art; at the same time, however, he had great admiration for his grandfather, whom he "would see sitting at his microscope day after day, engaged in the discovery of the gall capillaries of the liver". The result was long hesitation over the choice of his final subject of study. It was the First World War, with its attendant misery, that decided him to take up medicine. Heilmeyer studied at the university of his home town, Munich, where his teachers included Conrad Röntgen, Friedrich v. Müller, Ernst v. Romberg and Ferdinand Sauerbruch. In 1926, together with Veil, one of his teachers, he moved to the university of Jena where, as assistant and later as consultant, he prepared himself for his academic career, habilitating with a dissertation on urine pigment. He was led from research into haemoglobin and diseases of the blood, a large number of which he discovered, to work on iron metabolism. He was the first to recognize the significance of serum-iron and serum-copper in the diagnosis of diseases.

In 1946, after a year at Düsseldorf, Heilmeyer was appointed to a chair at Freiburg, where he set about re-developing the university medical hospital, with such great success that he has three times been offered, and has refused, a chair at Munich since that time. He continued his work in the field of haematology; the rapid development of the use of chemotherapy against infection, particularly in the cases of tuberculosis and cancer, provided fresh objects for his research. His books have been translated into a number of languages. Despite his success as a researcher, Heilmeyer has retained a passionate interest in practical medicine, and also sees it as his duty to train young doctors and pass on his knowledge to the next generation. In 1964 he was entrusted with the foundation of a new College of Science and Medicine at Ulm, whose Vice-Chancellor (Rektor) he became in 1965.

Ludwig Erhard

Ludwig Erhard was born at Fürth in Bavaria in 1897. He was to become a merchant like his father, and in 1913 began an apprenticeship at Nuremberg. He was called up in 1916, and was severely wounded near Ypres in 1918. After convalescing he began studying at the newly-founded College of Economic and Social Sciences at Nuremberg in 1919, where he completed the diploma course, then continued his studies at Frankfurt University. Here he first came into contact with Franz Oppenheimer, the sociologist and economist, and protagonist of liberal socialism, under whom he took his doctor's degree, and who later became his friend. "This man was a decisive influence in my life", confesses Erhard. (Oppenheimer died in exile in 1943.) At the end of 1928 Erhard became assistant to Vershofen at the "Institute for Market Research and Analysis" at Nuremberg, and shortly afterwards his deputy. He abandoned his intention of habilitating at the College at Nuremberg after 1933, and specialized in market research, making a name for himself in professional and business circles. In 1942 he gave up his post to found a private research institute. It was at this time that he composed a memorandum for Goerdeler on "Economic and Financial Reconstruction after the Collapse". In his political testament, Goerdeler addressed to his friends the remark: "Erhard will give you sound advice". In 1945 a copy of this memorandum fell into the hands of the Americans, who invited Erhard to take up the post of Minister of Economics in Munich; in 1946 he left the government, and in 1947 became a professor at Munich University. He did the groundwork for the currency reform at the Agency "Money and Credit" at Bad Homburg. As director of the "Economic Administration" in Frankfurt, he was able to declare on 20th June 1948: "Henceforth the only ration card in the Federal Republic is the Deutsche Mark!" After his election to the first Bundestag Erhard became, in 1949, Federal Minister of Economics. It was his policy, which at first met with considerable resistance, that laid the foundations of the successful reconstruction of Western Germany. Since 1963 Erhard has been Federal Chancellor.

Theodor Eschenburg

Theodor Eschenburg comes of an old Lübeck family. His grandfather was Lord Mayor and a senator of the "Free Hanseatic City" of Lübeck. This grandfather was thus a colleague of Senator Buddenbrook, and Eschenburg's father's youngest brother went to school with Thomas Mann. His father was a naval officer. Born at Kiel in 1904, Theodor took his school-leaving examination in 1924 at the Katharineum Grammar School in Lübeck, and began his university studies at Tübingen. He studied in Berlin from 1926 to 1929, during which time he became friends with Stresemann. In 1928 he obtained his doctor's degree, with a dissertation on "The Empire at the Crossroads–Bassermann, Bülow and the Block". He was one of the founders of the Staatspartei (State Party). In 1933 he retired from politics, and became manager of associations within the hardware and haberdashery industries. In 1945 Carlo Schmid invited him to take up the post of Commissioner for Refugees in the newly-formed government of Württemberg-Hohenzollern. He was removed from office in 1947 at the demand of the French authorities, but simultaneously appointed deputy to the Minister of the Interior. In 1949 the parliament (Landtag) of Württemberg-Hohenzollern called for disciplinary action against him for undue criticism of parliament and government, and demanded his dismissal; this demand was rejected by the government. In 1951 Eschenburg was appointed Staatsrat (Councillor of State). Since 1952 he has held a full professorship in politics at Tübingen University. From 1961 to 1963 Eschenburg was Vice-Chancellor (Rektor) of the university. The best known of his works are "Herrschaft der Verbände?" (Dictatorship of Pressure Groups?) (1955), "Ämterpatronage" (Patronage in Office) (1961), "Staat und Gesellschaft in Deutschland" (State and Society in Germany) (1962). "Die improvisierte Demokratie" (The Improvised Democracy) (1963), and "Über Autorität" (On Authority) (1965). The two volumes of "Zur politischen Praxis in der Bundesrepublik" (Political Practice in the Federal Republic) were published in 1964 and 1966.

Carlo Schmid

The son of a German father and a French mother, Carlo Schmid was born at Perpignan in 1896, and spent his boyhood in both France and Germany.

After the war he studied international law at Tübingen, where he expressed his political commitment by the foundation of a student socialist group; his "intellectual pride", however, he has said, forbade him to join the Social Democratic Party. He became a judge at the petty sessions (Landgericht) at Tübingen, then head of a department at the Kaiser Wilhelm Institute for Foreign Civil and International Law in Berlin, and worked at international courts of arbitration in The Hague and Paris, being fascinated by not only the philosophical, but also the practical problems of international law. In 1929 he habilitated at Tübingen, but was unable subsequently to take up a chair, as he refused to have anything to do with the Nazi movement.

After the Second World War Schmid became the first head of the government of the reorganized Land of Württemberg-Hohenzollern, and re-founder of the Social Democratic Party in this Land, although at the time of its foundation he was not a member of the party. Since 1947 he has been a member of the executive committee of the Socialist Party.

Schmid has been Vice-President of the German Bundestag since 1949, a member of the Council of Europe since 1950, and President of the Western European Union since 1963.

Since 1953 Schmid has held the chair of political science at the University of Frankfurt-on-Main, having held the chair of civil law at Tübingen for the previous seven years. His favourites among his own books are his translation of Baudelaire's "Les Fleurs du Mal", and "Politik und Geist" (Politics and Intellectual Life).

Golo Mann

Golo Mann, the historian, was born in Munich in 1909, the son of Thomas and Katia Mann. He attended Salem School, of which Kurt Hahn was headmaster, and where he took his school-leaving examination in 1927. In 1932 he took his doctor's degree at Heidelberg under Jaspers. From 1933 to 1936 he was Lecteur in German literature and history at the École Normale Supérieure at St. Cloud, and at Rennes University, in France. From 1937 to 1940 he edited the magazine "Mass und Wert" (Proportions and Values), published by his father in Zurich. In 1942 and 1943 he taught modern history at Olivet College, Olivet, Michigan, then at Claremont Men's College, Claremont, California. After a spell as visiting professor at Münster in Westphalia, Mann held the chair of political science at the College of Technology at Stuttgart from 1960 to 1963. He now lives as a free-lance writer at Kilchberg, near Zurich.

In 1963 Mann was awarded the City of Berlin Fontane Prize, and in 1964 the City of Mannheim Schiller Prize.

Among his many publications the following deserve especial mention: "Friedrich von Gentz" (1947), and "The History of Germany in the 19th and 20th Centuries" (1950). Golo Mann is editor and author of several chapters of the "History of the World" (11 vols.) published by the Propylaea Press (1960–1965).

140

Hans Mayer

Hans Mayer, who was born at Cologne in 1907, studied law and political science, modern history and philosophy. Among his teachers were Max Scheler and Nicolai Hartmann, Hans Kelsen, who taught philosophy of law, Helmuth Plessner and Friedrich Meinecke. In 1931 Mayer took his doctor's degree at Cologne with a dissertation on political theory. From 1933 to 1945 he lived in exile in Strasbourg, Paris, Geneva and Zurich. Research grants from institutions in America and Switzerland enabled him to continue work on his book "Georg Büchner and his Age". In 1945 he returned to Germany, where he became chief producer at Radio Frankfurt, later known as Hessischer Rundfunk (Hesse Radio), then lecturer in sociology and cultural history at the Akademie der Arbeit (Academy of Work) in Frankfurt; in 1948 he took up an appointment as professor at the University of Leipzig, where he held the chair of modern German literature and world literature until 1963, in which year he moved to West Germany. Since then he has accepted numerous invitations to lecture abroad, among others those to the universities of Rome, Paris, Stockholm, Uppsala, Helsinki and Oslo. In the summer term of 1965, he was visiting professor at the Technical University in Berlin, after which he took up the chair of German language and literature at the Hanover College of Technology.

Hans Mayer has made his name as a literary historian, essayist and critic. He has written about Georg Büchner, Thomas Mann, Richard Wagner and Bertolt Brecht, essays on the German Classics and Romantics, and on international developments in modern literature. His works have been translated into many languages. He has edited a highly-regarded three-volume anthology of "Masterpieces of German Literary Criticism", and translated from the French, among other things, Jean-Paul Sartre's autobiography "Les Mots". Mayer is a member of the Berlin Academy of the Arts, the PEN Club, and the German jury for the International Literature Prize.

Walter Jens

Walter Jens was born in Hamburg in 1923. After attending the Johanneum Grammar School there, he studied classics and German literature at Hamburg and Freiburg. In 1949 he wrote his first book, "Nein – die Welt der Angeklagten" (No – the World of the Accused), after taking up a lectureship at Tübingen University, and from then until 1957 four more novels, including the story about the theatre world "Vergessene Gesichter" (Forgotten Faces) (1952), the novellen "The Blind Man" (1951) and "Das Testament des Odysseus" (The Testament of Odysseus) (1957) and the radio play "Ahasver". During the last ten years Jens has departed more and more in his writings from mere story-telling and, in his endeavour to arrive at valid statements in the field of his studies, and to pass them on to his students and readers, has striven to combine fiction and scholarship in essays and treatises, parables and formal addresses. His development along these lines has been marked by the publication of the books "Statt einer Literaturgeschichte" (Instead of a History of Literature) (1957), and "Zueignungen" (Dedications) (1962), and, more important, the travel book "Die Götter sind sterblich" (The Gods are Mortal) (1959), and "Herr Meister", a "Dialogue about a Novel" (1963). Since his appointment to the newly-created chair of classics and rhetoric at Tübingen University, Jens has had an ideal opportunity of combining his interests as an author with those of the teacher, in his double function as writer and scholar, teacher and rhetorician.

Walter Höllerer

Walter Höllerer was born at Sulzbach-Rosenberg in Bavaria in 1922. After leaving school he began to study theology, then changed to German literature, philosophy, history and comparative literature. In 1952 he published his first poems. In 1954 he became co-editor of the magazine "Akzente" and in 1961 editor of "Sprache im technischen Zeitalter" (Language in the Age of Technology). He took up a lectureship at the University of Frankfurt-on-Main, then a chair of literature at the Technical University in Berlin. He has travelled abroad as visiting professor and lecturer, mainly in the U.S.A., at the universities of Harvard, Princeton, Chapel Hill, Columbia (New York) and Madison (Wisconsin). He has published works of literary scholarship such as "Zwischen Klassik und Moderne. Lachen und Weinen in der Dichtung einer Übergangszeit", critical essays and fiction, edited anthologies such as "Transit", a book of mid-century poetry, "Movens", records and analyses of modern literature, art and music (together with Franz Mon and Manfred de la Motte), and "Junge amerikanische Lyrik" (Recent American Poetry). Höllerer is head of the Institute for Language and Literature in Berlin. Of himself he writes: "In my studies of literature and teaching at universities I have tried not to content myself with points of view which I considered unsatisfactory; such notions, I have discovered, are more persistent than one tends to think".

Eduard Berend

Eduard Berend, who was born at Hanover in 1883 of a long-established Jewish family, studied German literature, and took his doctor's degree at Munich University in 1907 with a dissertation on the aesthetics of Jean Paul. During the following years, Berend was mainly occupied with research on Jean Paul's vast literary remains at the Prussian State Library in Berlin. From 1915 to 1918 he fought on the Western front in the infantry, where he eventually attained the rank of company commander. In 1925, for the centenary of Jean Paul's death, Berend was entrusted with the preparation of a historical and critical edition of the writer's complete works, estimated to run to 40 volumes, of which 33 have appeared so far. Thus Jean Paul has remained Berend's chief preoccupation throughout his life. While in exile, Berend lived in Geneva. Since 1957 he has been in charge of the Jean Paul Archives at the National Schiller Museum at Marbach. In 1963 he received an honorary doctorate of the Free University of Berlin.

Benno v. Wiese

Looking back upon his life, Benno v. Wiese states that he probably owes the best of his teaching and writing in the fields of the history of ideas and literary interpretation to Karl Jaspers and Friedrich Gundolf, his "unforgettable teachers". "In my books", he writes, "I have tried to establish communication from mind to mind over centuries past and to persuade the reader to participate in this communication. I do not press any ingenious theories or modern slogans on him; all I want is to arouse the reader's interest and to draw him, before he knows it, into a discussion obliging him to absorb all that is great in German literature and the German language, as if it were an immediate challenge in our own day."

Benno v. Wiese was born in Frankfurt-on-Main in 1903. He studied philosophy, German literature and sociology, qualifying as a university teacher under Oskar Walzel in 1929. He taught German literature first at Bonn University, from 1932 to 1943 at Erlangen, then at Münster. Since 1957 he has held a chair at the University of Bonn. His main works are "German Tragedy from Lessing to Hebbel" (1948), "Eduard Mörike" (1950), "Friedrich Schiller" (1959), and "The German Novelle from Goethe to Kafka" (1956 and 1960).

Emil Preetorius

Emil Preetorius, who was born at Mainz in 1883, has spent a long life "cœur à cœur with art". He completed his university studies of science and history of art, soon after the turn of the century, by "resolutely and prosaically", as he puts it, acquiring his state examination and doctorate in law, then hurried to Munich, to devote himself henceforth to art. Apart from a short spell at the Academy of Art, he was mainly self-taught. The first book which he illustrated, in 1906, was Chamisso's "Peter Schlemihl", and many more followed, together with work in other fields of commercial art, such as posters, book jackets, signets and lettering. Seventeen years after "Peter Schlemihl", at the instigation of Bruno Walter and Thomas Mann, he designed his first stage scenery, for the production of Gluck's "Iphigenia in Aulis" at the National Theatre in Munich; later he was to design scenery for almost every European opera stage of note. In 1931 he was appointed stage designer at Bayreuth, where he tackled the problem of developing a new style of Wagnerian décor. He began his career as a teacher of art early, at the College of Book Illustration and Commercial Art which he founded with Paul Renner in Munich in 1909, and in 1910 he also took charge of the city and state schools of commercial art. In 1925 he was offered a post at the Munich Academy as a teacher of book illustration and stage design. It was about 1900, in Berlin, that Preetorius first became acquainted with the art of East Asia, and laid the foundations of a collection whose importance has won it European renown. Preetorius has received a number of honours, including honorary doctorates of the unversities of Munich, Mainz and Giessen. With the passage of the years, he has cut down the number of posts which he holds, but is still president of the Bavarian Academy of Fine Arts.

Kurt Hahn

While still at school in Berlin, where he was born in 1886, Kurt Hahn was already planning to found a school of his own some day, on a basis of mutual trust between teachers and pupils. At the age of sixteen he became acquainted with the ideas of Hermann Lietz, which made a deep impression on him. He studied classics at Oxford and Göttingen. In 1916, during the First World War, in the course of efforts to bring about a peace by negotiation, he first met Prince Max of Baden, whose private secretary he became in 1918, after the Prince's resignation as Chancellor. It was from their common concern with youth in the years after the war that the decision to found a new school arose; it was established in the former Cistercian monastery of Salem, near Lake Constance.

The principles of the Salem education sprang from four main sources: Plato's theories on man, Goethe's "Pädagogische Provinz", Hermann Lietz's ideas, and the practice of the English public schools. The founder aimed to give moral education a predominant place in the programme of the school. The main difference between the "school republic" of Salem and other boarding-schools is the sharing of responsibility throughout the community.

In 1933 Hahn was forced to emigrate, and with the help of friends founded at Gordonstoun in Scotland an "English Salem" which already had 175 pupils by the outbreak of the Second World War.

In 1955, together with Sir Lawrance Darvall, Hahn developed plans for an international school, at which pupils of all races and tongues would be educated in an atmosphere of understanding and trust; the first "Atlantic College" of this kind was founded in 1962 in South Wales.

Kurt Hahn has received honorary doctorates from several universities. He now lives mostly at Hermannsberg, near Pfullendorf, in the immediate neighbourhood of one of the Salem junior schools, and follows the life of his schools with keen interest.

Gustav Stein

Gustav Stein's ancestors on his mother's side were natives of the Bergisches Land; his great-grandfather was a member of the Prussian National Assembly. It is possible that Stein inherited his passions for politics and art from his father's art-loving family on the one hand, and the politically-minded maternal side of the family on the other; at any rate Stein, who was born at Duisburg in 1903, is not only a man of the world, being a trained lawyer and manager of a number of industrial associations, but is just as much at home in the world of art—the art, moreover, not only of Europe, but also of the other continents.

It was from the conviction that the furtherance of the arts is an important task in modern society, that personal contact between the individual and the artist must be re-established in this age of mass culture, and that business enterprises must be persuaded to commission works of art that the Cultural Committee of the Federal Association of German Industry came into being; Theodor Heuss has said in its praise that it has played an essential part in West German cultural life during the last decade. It is thanks to Gustav Stein and Hermann Reusch, the spiritual fathers and promoters of this Cultural Committee, that the initiative of private enterprise in the Federal Republic has been harnessed to the promotion and propagation of artistic creativity, and that the resulting patronage of the arts has not favourised any particular trend in art or literature. Stein now holds a chair at the State Academy of Art at Düsseldorf. He is also a member of the Federal Parliament.

Hugo Friedrich

Hugo Friedrich was born at Karlsruhe in 1904, and began with the study of German literature, philosophy and the history of art, but changed, under the influence of Karl Vossler, to what he calls "the spacious, colourful and congenial world" of Romance languages and literature. Among his teachers were Ernst Robert Curtius, C. Neumann, Karl Jaspers and Friedrich Gundolf. After taking his finals, he became a grammar-school teacher for a time. In 1934 he habilitated, with a dissertation on anti-Romantic thought in modern France. Travel brought him into contact with the living realities of the Romance world. Since 1937 he has been professor of Romance languages and literature at Freiburg, having meanwhile refused a number of offers of appointments elsewhere.

About the aims of his research Friedrich writes: "The history of literature, at least until the middle of the 18th century, is the history, not of private individuals, but of the creative artist; not of personal fortunes, but of suprapersonal ideas; not of diaries, but of the imagination, themes, styles. This may sound exaggerated, but we have often in the past been guilty of a facile romanticising of European literature; for some decades now research has tended to counteract this tendency, and this new movement has my support". Friedrich has won fame with his book "Die Struktur der modernen Lyrik" (The Structure of Modern Poetry) (1956). His latest work is entitled "Epochen der italienischen Lyrik" (A History of Italian Poetry) (1964).

Wolfgang Schadewaldt

Since 1950 Wolfgang Schadewaldt has been professor of classics and the classical influence on European literature at Tübingen University. His main fields are the literature and philosophy of early and classical Greece, and Goethe.

The son of a doctor, Otto Schadewaldt, he was born in 1900 in Berlin, where he studied classics, German literature and archaeology, mainly under Werner Jaeger and Ulrich v. Wilamowitz-Möllendorff. After taking his doctor's degree and habilitating, he became professor of classics at the universities of Königsberg (1928), Freiburg (1929), Leipzig (1934) and Berlin (1941). There, in 1947, he initiated the production of the "Goethe Dictionary", with research groups in Berlin, Hamburg and Tübingen (working under the auspices of the Academies of Berlin, Göttingen and Heidelberg); the stage has now been reached where publication of the first instalment of the five-volume work is expected during 1966. Schadewaldt's best-known works include the "Ilias-Studien" (Studies on the Iliad), "Von Homers Welt und Werk" (On the Works and World of Homer), "Hellas und Hesperien" (essays on Hellenic and Occidental literature), and the "Goethe-Studien" (Goethe Studies). In recent years Schadewaldt has become well-known for his translations of the Odyssey, "The Persians" and "Seven against Thebes" of Aeschylus, Sophocles's "Antigone", "Electra", "Oedipus Rex", and "Ajax", Aristophanes's "Lysistrata" and "The Birds", and Menander's "The Arbitration", which have been performed at a number of theatres in Germany, and broadcast on radio and television. They were published together in 1964, in a volume entitled "Griechisches Theater" (Greek Drama). Professor Schadewaldt is a member of various learned societies and academies at home and abroad, and the recipient of numerous honours, including membership of the Order Pour le Mérite for Arts and Science.

Josef Eberle

Josef Eberle was born in 1901 at Rottenburg-on-Neckar, the Sumelocenna of the Romans, the son of the town clerk; he attended grammar school at Tübingen, where he served his apprenticeship as a bookseller at Heckenhauer's, the famous old-established bookshop (at the same desk, incidentally, at which Hermann Hesse had checked invoices fifteen years previously). Eberle worked in bookshops in Berlin, Karlsruhe, Stuttgart, Baden-Baden and Leipzig. From 1929 until March 1933 he was in charge of radio talks at the Süddeutscher Rundfunk (South German Broadcasting System) in Stuttgart, working at the same time as a free-lance journalist. In 1933, he was dismissed from the broadcasting service, not least because of his wife's being Jewish; he worked at the American Consulate-General in Stuttgart until diplomatic relations between Germany and the U.S.A. were broken off, then as a librarian with an insurance company, writing in his spare time, although none of his work could be published. Since September 1945 Eberle has been publisher of the "Stuttgarter Zeitung"; he is, as he says, "still passionately devoted" to his work on this paper, "in order to be able to contribute at least a little to ensuring that history does not repeat itself".

Eberle has become well-known as a poet in the local dialect of Swabia, under the pseudonym of 'Sebastian Blau'. At the same time as, under the Nazis, he was forbidden to write, his works, "through no fault of his own, were canonized by incorporation into school readers". Later he took refuge from the confines of his dialect in the universality of Latin, "for fear of becoming a professional Swabian"; he has to his credit several volumes of Latin poetry and essays on the Roman world, "for which he has been crowned Poet Laureate by the classical scholars of Tübingen".

Eberle describes as the greatest stroke of luck he has had the fact that he was able to acquire the so-called Cotta Archives for the "Stuttgarter Zeitung", and present them to the National Schiller Museum at Marbach.

Walter Schulz

Walter Schulz's field of research is the history of metaphysics. He analyses the development of man's conception of God, endeavouring in the light of this investigation to arrive at a new understanding of the various movements in modern philosophy. In his interpretation of the later Schelling he has drawn a new picture of German Idealism. With insight into the importance of metaphysics in the philosophy of past ages he combines the recognition of the dead end at which metaphysics has now arrived. The question which governs his thinking is thus what part philosophy can still play in an antimetaphysical world. Schulz, who was born at Gnadenfeld in Upper Silesia in 1912, the son of a parson, attended the Zinzendorf Grammar School at Niesky, where he took his school-leaving examination in 1933. He studied philosophy, theology and classics at Marburg, Breslau and Leipzig, and in 1943 took his doctor's degree, with a dissertation on "Soul and Being. Interpretations of Plato's Phaidon". In 1951 he habilitated under Hans-Georg Gadamer at Heidelberg, and since 1955 has been professor of philosophy at Tübingen University. His main publications are a study of Heidegger's position in modern thought (1953–1954), "Die Vollendung des Deutschen Idealismus in der Spätphilosophie Schellings" (The Culmination of German Idealism in the Later Philosophy of Schelling) (1955), "Der Gott der neuzeitlichen Metaphysik" (The God of Modern Metaphysics) (1957), and "J. G. Fichte, Vernunft und Freiheit" (J. G. Fichte, Reason and Liberty) (1962).

Hans-Georg Gadamer

Gadamer is numbered among the thinkers who have laid the foundations of a new conception of history; for him, as for Hegel, Dilthey and Heidegger, the way to truth is through the study of history. It is this idea that lies behind the two main themes which occupy Gadamer: the tracing of the origins of our own ideas in Greek thought, and the examination of historical truth in its most spontaneous and natural form, poetical writing.

Hans-Georg Gadamer was born at Marburg in 1900. In 1918 he took his school-leaving examination at the Holy Spirit Grammar School at Breslau, where he grew up. He studied German literature, history, philosophy, history of art and classics, and obtained his doctor's degree under Paul Natorp. In 1929 he habilitated under Martin Heidegger at Marburg. In 1939 he became professor of philosophy at Leipzig University, whose Vice-Chancellor (Rektor) he was in 1946–47. Since 1949 he has taught at Heidelberg, as the successor of Karl Jaspers. Gadamer is editor of the journal "Philosophische Rundschau," co-editor of the series "Kant Studies" and "Hegel Studies", president of the Allgemeine Gesellschaft für Philosophie in Deutschland (Philosophical Association of Germany) and the Internationale Vereinigung zur Förderung des Studiums der Hegelschen Philosophie (International Society for the Advancement of Hegelian Studies). His main work, "Wahrheit und Methode. Grundzüge einer philosophischen Hermeneutik"(Truth and Method. The Principles of Philosophical Hermeneutics) appeared in 1960.

Arnold Metzger

Arnold Metzger was born at Landau in the Palatinate in 1892, took his grammar school leaving examination (Abitur) there in 1910, and obtained his doctor's degree at Jena as early as 1914, under Rudolf Eucken. The same year he volunteered for active military service, and in 1917 was captured by the Russians, while an officer concerned with German-Bulgarian espionage. He was detained in Eastern Siberia until the spring of 1918, when he escaped right across Asiatic and European Russia in the guise of a Russian peasant, carrying his mattress on his back. From 1918 to 1920 he worked at the Reichszentrale für Heimatdienst (the 'Centre for Political Education') in Berlin together with Max Scheler, Radbruch, the lawyer, and the architect Peter Behrens. In 1920 he was invited to Freiburg by Husserl, whose assistant he remained until 1924. In 1925 appeared Metzger's "Der Gegenstand der Erkenntnis" (The Object of Cognition), which brought him into conflict with the ideas of Husserl. In 1933 followed "Phänomenologie und Metaphysik" (Phenomenology and Metaphysics). It was in this year that the continuation of Metzger's academic career was made impossible for him, and in 1938 he finally emigrated to Paris; when France was occupied by Germany he crossed to England from Dinard, disguised as a Breton fisherman. In 1941 he went to the U.S.A., where he was invited to lecture at the universities of Yale, Harvard, and Columbia, and was later appointed to a lectureship at Simmons College, Boston.

Since 1952 Metzger has taught at the University of Munich. In 1955 appeared his "Freiheit und Tod" (Freedom and Death), in 1964 "Dämonie und Transzendenz" (The Demonic and the Transcendent) and in 1966 "Die Philosophie der Gesellschaft im gegenwärtigen Zeitalter" (The Philosophy of Society in the Present Age). Metzger's thought is concerned with the changing nature of man in the changing society of our time; a society which has forgotten its original knowledge of the inner transcendence of existence is faced with the problem of regaining the freedom of the individual.

Ernst Bloch

The philosophical thinking of Bloch, as a young man, was first formed by the teachings of Hegel and the Hegelians, Schelling, the Romantic nature philosophers, and Schopenhauer. The first expression of his lively thought and alert contemporaneity was the work "Geist der Utopie" (The Spirit of Utopia), which was published in Munich in 1918; the basic theme of this first work was taken up again in a more definite, deromanticized manner in the book "Das Prinzip Hoffnung" (The Principle of Hope), written during Bloch's years of exile in America: man as a creature unconquered, and therefore erect, and therefore hopeful. The historical and contemporary manifestations of life, art, religion, and thought are explained against the background of this Utopian goal, in the light of which man is seen as the creature bearing the full responsibility for what becomes of this world, and for making it a place inhabited by free, fraternally-minded men, his "home".

Ernst Bloch was born at Ludwigshafen-on-Rhine in 1885, studied philosophy, physics and music at Munich and Würzburg, obtained his doctor's degree in 1908, and then lived for some years as a free-lance writer. In 1933 he emigrated, first to Switzerland, then to the United States; at the request of the Romance scholar Werner Krauss, he returned to Germany in 1949 to take up a chair of philosophy at Leipzig. Some of his pupils were arrested in connection with the events in Hungary in 1956, and he himself was forced to retire. In August 1961 he failed to return to Leipzig from a visit to West Germany, and since then has lived and taught at Tübingen.

Karl Jaspers

"My writings are governed by the will to do what I can to increase, by however little, the amount of understanding in the world, and to do so by making the reader uneasy, by opening his eyes to the potentialities of his existence, by encouraging him to become himself, and by casting him up on the shores of the uncomprehended." Thus reads a passage from the "Philosophical Autobiography" which Jaspers published in 1953. His philosophical system has political and didactic tendencies; he sees it as his task to help people, in particular the Germans, to a more complete self-awareness, free from the arrogance that has caused so much mischief in the past.

Karl Jaspers was born at Oldenburg in 1883. His father, who had studied law, was a senior civil servant, and later director of a bank; his mother came of a family of farmers from Butjadingen. Jaspers attended grammar school at Oldenburg, and soon found himself in conflict with the authoritarian school system and its out-of-date methods. At seventeen he read the works of Spinoza, who became "his philosopher". After taking his school-leaving examination, he studied law for 3 semesters, then medicine, took his medical finals in 1908, and was an assistant at the psychiatric clinic at Heidelberg University for a time afterwards. In 1913 he habilitated, and became a lecturer in psychology in the faculty of arts at Heidelberg; in 1921 he obtained a full professorship in philosophy. All the decisions in his life have been influenced by the fact that he has been an invalid from childhood; the necessary consequence of this has been the determination carefully to husband and direct his energies. In 1907 he met Gertrud Mayer, who later became his wife; she came of a long-established Jewish family from the Mark Brandenburg. In 1933 began years of hardship and distress for Jaspers; in 1937 he was deprived of his chair, and was forbidden to publish any of his writings from 1938 onwards. His experiences during the twelve years of Nazi rule led to an "estrangement from Germany in its political aspect"; by contrast, he valued the more highly "the natural, unquestioned German-ness" of his language, family origins and homeland. It was at his instigation that the re-founding of the University of Heidelberg, after the occupation of the town by the Americans, came about.

"My philosophical task was now the elucidation of the moral and realistic considerations involved in politics, and to take the standpoint of a hypothetical world citizen as the basis for my political thinking." Thus Jaspers describes his attitude at the end of the Second World War. In 1948 he took up a chair at the University of Basle, where he now lives. Jaspers has been awarded the City of Frankfurt Goethe Prize and the German Publishers' Peace Prize.

Martin Heidegger

Martin Heidegger writes: "In 1907 a friend of the family, Dr. Conrad Gröber, later Archbishop of Freiburg, showed me Franz Brentano's dissertation, dating from 1862, entitled "Von der mannigfachen Bedeutung des Seienden nach Aristoteles" (The Manifold Meaning of Being in the Works of Aristotle). On the title page Brentano had written a phrase from Aristotle, which I have translated thus: 'The existent becomes evident (with regard to Being) in many ways'. In this sentence is contained the question which has governed my whole thought: what is the simple, comprehensive definition of Being which covers all its manifold meanings?" In "Being and Time" (1927) the first part of the answer became apparent. For the many who mistakenly interpreted this book as a work of philosophical anthropology, or even an attempt "to proclaim a nihilistic and heroic conception of man", there were for a long time few who had the insight to see that thinking was confronted here with a question which had never been put before. "We must no longer inquire about the single existent, but about Being as such, from which the existent derives its meaning. For this meaning has always been accessible, even if unconsciously, to the human comprehension of Being. Accordingly, it was necessary to begin by interpreting the

nature of man with reference to the basic structures of the comprehension of Being, as human existence (Dasein) in history.

Martin Heidegger was born at Messkirch in Baden in 1889, the son of a sacristan and master-cooper. He attended grammar school at Konstanz and Freiburg, and began to study theology at Freiburg in 1909. The two volumes of Husserl's "Logische Untersuchungen" (Logical Studies) were on his desk in the seminary from the first day onwards. After four terms Heidegger decided to devote himself wholly to philosophy, which made it necessary for him to engage in the study of the arts and the natural sciences. In 1916 Husserl came to Freiburg, and Heidegger became his assistant in 1919. Practice in phenomenological "seeing", which only became possible for Heidegger in the years of personal contact with his eminent teacher, formed the basis for his attempt to elucidate the troubling question of Being, by way of an interpretation of the history of Western thought. In 1923 Heidegger was appointed to a chair at Marburg, and in 1928 returned to Freiburg. He refused two offers of appointments at the University of Berlin in 1930 and 1933. In May 1933 he was unanimously elected Vice-Chancellor (Rektor) of Freiburg University, but as early as February 1934 he resigned under protest, refusing to take part in the customary ceremony of handing over office, thereby testifying to his political error. He became professor emeritus in 1951.

In his examination of Western metaphysics, the religious testimonies of Pascal, Luther and Kierkegaard, in his interest in early Greek thought, the poetry of Hölderlin and Trakl, and in his interpretation of Nietzsche, Heidegger's concern has always been with the attempt to awaken and express in language the experience of the peculiarity and the transformation of Being in the sense of presence. In his "Letter on Humanism" (to his friend Jean Beaufret) he says: "Henceforth thinking will no longer be philosophy, because it will think more originally than metaphysics (another name for philosophy). But future thought cannot, as Hegel demanded, lay aside the name 'love of wisdom' and become wisdom itself in the form of absolute knowledge. Thinking is on the descent to the poverty of its preliminary nature."

Rudolf Bultmann

Rudolf Bultmann lives at Marburg, where he taught the New Testament from 1921 to 1951. He joined the movement of "dialectical theology", the beginning of which was marked by the appearance in 1919 of Karl Barth's commentary on the Epistle to the Romans, because he had realized that theology should not regard Christian belief as a phenomenon belonging to the history of ideas, but that this belief is the response of man to the word of God, and that theology must deal with this word and with man, to whom it is addressed. However, Bultmann endeavoured at the same time to keep alive the traditions of the historical and critical method of "liberal theology" in which he had begun, and to apply them to modern theological views. The key-word of the theological controversy which he inaugurated is "Entmythologisierung" (de-mythologizing), which he used for the first time in 1941. His years at Marburg were marked by intensive exchanges of ideas with his colleagues in the theological faculty, and with theologians from elsewhere, such as Karl Barth and Friedrich Gogarten. His encounters with Martin Heidegger had a decisive influence on him.

Rudolf Bultmann is the son of a parson, and was born at Wiefelstede, near Oldenburg, in 1884; his ancestors were farmers. After taking his school-leaving examination at Oldenburg, he began his theological studies at Tübingen, continuing them at Berlin and Marburg. Among his teachers were the church historian Karl Müller, Hermann Gunkel, who was professor of Old Testament studies, Adolf Harnack, whose field was the history of dogma, the New Testament scholars Adolf Jülicher and Johannes Weiss, and the professor of dogmatics Wilhelm Hermann. In 1916 Bultmann received his first offer of a chair, at Breslau; in the autumn of 1920 he moved to Giessen, and one year later to the University of Marburg, where he has remained until the present.

Gerhard Ebeling

Gerhard Ebeling is a Protestant theologian. He was born in Berlin in 1912. After taking his grammar school leaving examination, he began in 1930 to study theology under R. Bultmann, H. Frhr. v. Soden, and E. Brunner, among others, and philosophy under G. Krüger, E. Grisebach and N. Hartmann, at Marburg, Zurich and Berlin. In the autumn of 1934 he entered himself for examination by the illegal examination board of the Consistory of the "Confessing Church" of Berlin-Brandenburg. For eighteen months Ebeling served as a curate at Crossen-on-Oder and Fehrbellin, then attended the seminary of the Confessing Church at Finkenwalde, near Stettin, of which Dietrich Bonhoeffer was in charge. At Bonhoeffer's instigation he was given leave to go to Zurich to work for the degree of Doctor of Theology, which he obtained in 1938. After his second examination in theology, and ordination in Berlin-Dahlem, he became pastor of the emergency congregation of the Confessing Church in Berlin-Hermsdorf. From 1940 to 1945 he served in the army as a medical orderly. In August 1945 he began as assistant to H. Rückert at Tübingen University, habilitated, and in 1946 became professor of church history, being appointed to the chair of dogmatics in 1954. In 1956 he went to the University of Zurich to take up the chair of dogmatics, history of dogma and symbolism, returning to Tübingen in 1965. He has numerous publications to his credit, dealing mainly with his special fields, Luther studies, dogmatics and hermeneutics, and is a member of the commission for the publication of the standard edition of Luther's works.

Hanns Lilje

Almost every Sunday sees Hanns Lilje, the Bishop of the Lutheran Church of Hanover, in the pulpit. It is not only for his plain, clear language that he is highly esteemed as a preacher, but also for his keen understanding of present-day human problems. He contrives to combine piety with a sympathetic understanding of the questions of the modern world.

Hanns Lilje was born at Hanover in 1899. He studied theology and history of art at the universities of Göttingen, Leipzig and Zurich, obtaining the degree of Doctor of Theology. After taking his examinations, he became chaplain to the College of Technology in his native city, and in 1926 secretary of the German Student Christian Movement in Berlin. In 1928 he became a member of the executive committee of the Student Christian Movement, of which he became Vice-President in 1932. Having a flair for languages, Lilje took his interpreter's diploma in Berlin, thereby laying open the way to further oecumenical posts. In 1935 he was elected secretary of the Lutheran World Convention. Meanwhile the situation in Germany had become critical; Lilje was among the undaunted preachers of the Confessional Church, and in August 1944 he was arrested by the Gestapo, and sentenced by the so-called "People's High Court"; the end of the war brought his release from imprisonment.

In 1947 Lilje was unanimously elected Bishop by the convocation of the Church of Hanover. Years of reconstruction followed. The bishop preached in country parishes whose parsons were still prisoners of war, gave lectures, organized conferences, and founded the Lutheran Academy at Hermannsburg, which was lated moved to Loccum. He also established the weekly paper "Sonntagsblatt", an important organ of Lutheran opinion. From 1952 to 1957 he was president of the Lutheran World Federation.

Karl Rahner

Karl Rahner is professor of Christian thought and the philosophy of religion at the University of Munich, where he succeeded Romano Guardini. He was born at Freiburg-im-Breisgau in 1904, the son of a grammar-school teacher. He grew up as one of seven children, and is proud of his Alemannian descent, saying that he ascribes to the people of the Black Forest qualities which he would like to possess himself. He received his secondary education at the Realgymnasium in Freiburg, where he was "not a very keen" pupil. In 1922 he joined the Society of Jesus, and studied at Pullach, near Munich, and at Valkenburg in Holland. He was ordained in 1932. From 1934 to 1936 he was again in Freiburg, where he studied philosophy under Martin Heidegger, whom Rahner describes as an "unforgettable teacher". In 1937 he took up a lectureship in Catholic dogma at the University of Innsbruck, where his brother Hugo was teaching church history. The following year he was forbidden to continue teaching, and until 1945 worked as a parish priest in Vienna and Lower Bavaria. In 1949, after three years as a lecturer at the Jesuit College at Pullach, Rahner became professor of dogmatics at Innsbruck University, which in 1964 he left to take up his present post in Munich.

In his publications, Rahner is concerned with "theology in the broadest sense of the word"; theology, for him, is unthinkable without philosophy. His teachings and writings deal with the questions which daily arise in the life and thought of a Catholic, and which he seeks to answer not only with expert interpretation of dogma, but also with direct religious testimony.

Romano Guardini

Romano Guardini was born in 1885, of Italian parents, in Verona, which, situated where the Etsch valley opens into the plain of the Po, has guarded the military route from Italy to Germany from time immemorial. His family moved to Germany and, without ever losing his affection for the land of his birth, the young Guardini chose the Northern country as his home.

Guardini studied theology at Freiburg and Tübingen, and was ordained at Mainz in 1910.

After a number of years as a parish priest, he habilitated in Catholic theology at Bonn in 1922, and a year later was appointed by the Prussian Minister of Education, Becker, to the newly-established chair of philosophy of religion and Christian thought at the University of Berlin, where he taught until 1939, when the chair was abolished for political reasons. From then Guardini lived as a free-lance writer and lecturer until 1945, when he was offered a chair in the faculty of arts of Tübingen University; in 1948 he moved to Munich, where he taught until his retirement in 1964. His publications include not only philosophical and theological studies, but also works on literary history, and essays on educational and cultural policy. Guardini is a member of the Order Pour le Mérite for Arts and Science. In 1952 he was awarded the German Publishers' Peace Prize, and in 1962 the Erasmus Prize, Brussels.

Julius Döpfner

Julius Döpfner was born in 1913 at Hausen, near Bad Kissingen, in the attractive foothills of the Rhön mountains in Upper Franconia; his father worked as a porter at hotels in Bad Kissingen. Döpfner attended grammar school at Münnerstadt and Würzburg, where he took his school-leaving examination in 1933. One semester spent studying philosophy and theology at Würzburg–"unforgettable in those days of conflict and tension"–was followed by eight years in Rome, where Döpfner prepared for the ministry as a student at the Gregorian University of the Vatican. He was ordained in 1939, returning in the middle of the war to Germany, where he was parish priest at Grosswallstadt and Schweinfurt until 1944, subsequently becoming Subregens at the Seminary in Würzburg until his nomination as Bishop of Würzburg by Pope Pius XII in 1948.

During the years that followed Döpfner was concerned with the reconstruction of the badly damaged episcopal city, and pastoral reorientation, until in 1957 he was appointed successor of Bishop Wilhelm Weskamm in Berlin. Here he found himself faced with a totally different situation: the divided diocese, the problem of diaspora, and the threat of communism confronted him with fresh tasks. In 1958 Döpfner was admitted by Pope John XXIII to the College of Cardinals, and three years later designated Archbishop of Munich and Freising, his present office. He played an important part in the preparation and organisation of the Second Vatican Council.